CRITICAL JEWISH ISSUES

a Book for Teenagers

CRITICAL JEWISH ISSUES

a Book for Teenagers

by

Rabbi Ronald H. Isaacs

KTAV Publishing House, Inc.

Manufactured in the United States of America
ISBN 0-88125-587-4

Contents

I gratefully dedicate this book to
the students of Temple Sholom Hebrew High School.

*I have learned much from my teachers, even more
from my colleagues, but I have learned the most
from my students. (Talmud Ta'anit 7a)*

Acknowledgments

The author gratefully acknowledges permission to quote from the following sources:

Say Yes to Life, by Sidney Greenberg. Copyright © 1982 by Crown Publishers.

God in Search of Man, by Abraham Joshua Heschel. Copyright © 1995 by Harper and Row.

Derech Eretz: The Path to an Ethical Life, by Ronald Isaacs. Copyright © 1995 by the United Synagogue of Conservative Judaism, Department of Youth Activities.

The Condition of Life, Copyright ©1966, by the American Jewish Committee.

When Your Jewish Child Asks Why: Answers for Tough Questions, by Kerry M. Olitzky, Steven M. Rosman and David P. Kaskove. Copyright ©1993 by KTAV Publishing House, Inc.

Preface

During the past quarter-century, I have had the pleasure (in my capacity of rabbi) of working with and teaching hundreds of people from both my congregation and the community at large. One of the special joys and privileges of being the rabbi of Temple Sholom in Bridgewater, New Jersey, is the opportunity to teach teenagers in our Hebrew high school. On a weekly basis I am afforded a chance to try to arouse within the students an appreciation for the ideas and ideals of Judaism, while at the same time working to provide them with the necessary resources with which to actively contribute to Jewish community life in general, and to their own Jewish home lives in particular. I have also had a chance to learn a great deal from my students, including the pressing questions they ask that seem in need of special attention and clarification.

This book is an attempt to distill from my teaching experience those issues which I believe to be consistently ranked each year among the most interesting and challenging ones with which our students have grappled. It has always been my personal belief that what our Hebrew high school students most want to know and understand are the basic, fundamental concepts behind the issues they find most relevant to their lives. My own students, and I believe many others as well, are especially interested in knowing how they can make use of and apply Jewish principles and values in their personal decision-making. It has always been my teaching technique to try to create important and relevant reasons for students to use their Jewish knowledge in their immediate lives.

Throughout the centuries, beginning in biblical times, and extending through the rabbinic era into our own day, Judaism has had much to say by way of practical advice about the many problems and vital issues facing society. Its ethical, spiritual, and historical lessons continue to instruct and challenge us, as well as all people who are concerned with leading ethical lives.

It is with this in mind that I have written this book. It is my fervent hope that students and teachers will read it and be challenged. I want to thank all of my students and those in other communities whose commitment to Judaism and continuation of their Jewish education has served as a great source of inspiration to the community. May they continue to go forth from strength to strength, and may this book in some small way assist in helping them to change for the better the way in which they choose to live their lives.

A Note About Autonomy and Personal Choice:

Reform and Reconstructionist branches of Judaism afford free choice within the framework of Judaism and personal autonomy to follow that choice when it is made from a base of Jewish knowledge. Thus, several of the prescribed rituals discussed in this book may be more freely interpreted within the context of Reform and Reconstructionist decision-making.

Unit I
On Being Jewish

Introduction

For many Jews, religion seems to be an outmoded belief system that no longer fits their lives and is irrelevant to their concerns. For many others, Judaism is a life system that works to encourage spiritual awareness and a thirst for morality and justice. Why the disparity? Sometimes the difference between those who find Judaism antiquated and those who are energized by it is in the way in which it has been taught and "caught" both in the home as well as in the classroom.

My religious journey, in a sense, reminds me somewhat of that of our patriarch Abraham, who was told *lekh lekha*—go forth from your homeland and change the focus of your life. My journey back to Judaism began in 1960, two months before my thirteenth birthday and my Bar Mitzvah. It was then that my parents decided to send me to my first summer camping experience—Camp Ramah in Canada, a camp under the auspices of the Jewish Theological Seminary of America, headquarters for the Conservative movement. During this summer I witnessed (for the very first time) a community of several hundred enthusiastic people observing the holy Sabbath with song, dance, and intellectual stimulation. That summer, with its intensive Judaic study component conducted by stimulating teachers, led to my desire to begin to increase the observance of Shabbat in my home, my desire to continue to immerse myself in Jewish texts, and ultimately one of the most important of my life's decisions, that of deciding to become a rabbi!

For hundreds of years people like me have, through challenging study and learning, found Judaism a rich and holy path of living. This first chapter will examine four questions that are often asked of Jewish teenagers in their quest for Jewish knowledge:

1. Do we need organized religion?
2. Why should I be Jewish?
3. Does Judaism have essential principles and values that are valuable to me?
4. How can Judaism help me to make decisions in my life?

1
Do We Need Organized Religion?

Rabbi Mordecai Kaplan, the founder of the Reconstructionist movement, coined the phrase "Judaism as a civilization" and in 1934 published a book under that title. In it he proposed that Jews are more than just a religious group. They are a people, a community, who share a common heritage, one that includes history, a language, customs (folkways), and a great literature in addition to a religion.

Question

Do you agree or disagree with Kaplan's definition of Judaism? If you disagree, how would you define religion?

Whether or not you agree with Kaplan, it is clear from his definition that Judaism possesses a series of organized components, one of which is religion. Many have argued that we need organized religion for the same reason that we need organized political parties and other organized social movements. History has clearly demonstrated that in order for something to have an effect upon a community or the world at large, it is necessary for people to work together in a formal organization of some kind. Few politicians would be elected to public office without the backing of an organized body of supporters committed to the candidate's cause.

13

Centuries ago, the great sage Hillel: said, "Do not separate yourself from the community" (Pirke Avot 2:5). Since that time, Jewish people have always gathered together, not because they are all close friends or even because they agree with one another, but simply because they need to be organized with one another to go on being Jews.

There are, to be sure, people who believe that organization is undesirable in religion. Those who feel that religion ought to be a private matter and that no form of organization is necessitated see religion solely as pertaining to beliefs about God and prayer, with little bearing on one's daily routine. However, this view is far from the Jewish ideal. On the contrary, the Jewish ideal is summed up in the talmudic adage that "all Jews are responsible for one another" (Shevuot 39a). This principle also accounts for the many charitable activities that are part of every Jewish community.

Judaism has throughout its history been concerned with organizing people to help improve the quality of life in the world. The widespread support for the various United Jewish Appeal campaigns to bring oppressed Jews to Israel accents the tremendous commitment that many Jews feel in organizing to help their brothers and sisters throughout the world.

Exercises

1. Read the following quotations that relate to organized Jewish communal responsibilities. After reading them, share with your classmates some real-life examples of putting these quotations into action.

> When the community is in trouble, a person should not say, "I will go home and I will eat and drink and be at peace with myself."   (Talmud, Ta'anit 11a)

> A fast in which no Jewish sinners participate is no fast.
>   (Talmud Keritot 6b)

> We are One.   (UJA campaign slogan)

> All Israel are responsible for one another.
>   (Talmud Shevuot 39a)

2. What are some ways in which Jews help each other?

3. What unites Jews today? What divides them?

2
I'm a Jew:
Why Should I Be Jewish?

Someone once suggested a simple test by which we can assess the vitality of our Jewishness. "Imagine that you were followed for twenty-four hours. Would any of your actions indicate to the shadow that you were a Jew?"

Most Jews on any given day would likely fail this test. This is because many Jews do not see Judaism and Jewish values as speaking to them in their daily lives. Rather, our religion is often perceived as a pastime, something to which one may devote some time and effort, but surely not most of one's time, efforts, or resources. Judaism is lived as an adjunct to the really important things in life. This is because most Jews are unaware of the fact that Judaism is concerned with the most fundamental issues of meaning and purpose of one's very existence.

In a sense, Judaism begins with the call of our ancestor Abraham, who in Genesis 12:1 is told to go to a land that God will show him. God does not tell Abraham his ultimate destination, which makes it an even greater challenge. From the moment that Abraham accepts the challenge by going forth, he is destined to become the father of the Israelite nation.

16

Having become a Bar or Bat Mitzvah, it is now your responsibility to go forth and be a responsible person. Part of that responsibility is to fulfill the *mitzvot*, the special obligations that customarily begin to be performed by those who have become B'nai and B'not Mitzvah.

Throughout your Jewish education you have undoubtedly learned many "how-to" and cognitive facts related to being Jewish. But the question of why to be Jewish at all is rarely discussed. If you cannot answer the question "why be Jewish," then it is all the more likely that Judaism is playing a very minute role in your life.

Here are several ideas for your consideration. They were offered by several of my Hebrew high school students over the course of the last few years when they were asked to give me their thoughts on the question "why be Jewish." After reading them, see if you agree with any of their opinions.

1. One should be Jewish because God made a covenant with our people. Several thousand years ago, God told Moses to prepare the Israelites for a ceremony that would formalize their relationship to Him. God also made it known that the relationship would come with a condition. "If you will obey Me faithfully and keep My covenant, you shall be My treasured possession among all the peoples . . . you shall be to Me a kingdom of priests and a holy nation" (Exodus 19:5–6). Moses relayed God's messages to the elders of Israel, and the whole nation answered collectively, "All that God has spoken we will do" (Exodus 19:8). The covenant is a two-way relationship: We the Jewish people are to keep God's laws, and God is to watch over us.

2. One should be Jewish because Judaism can teach us how to improve the world and make it a better place in which to live.

3. One should be Jewish because Judaism is a way of living that promotes ethical and moral living.

4. One should be Jewish because we were given a beautiful tradition, and it is important to keep it alive and pass it on to those who will come after us.

5. One should be Jewish because we are part of a long and distinguished heritage. The Jewish people have survived over four thousand years in adverse conditions. Jews throughout that time have contributed enormously to the world in philosophy, ethics, science, and many other fields.

6. Knowing that you are Jewish is something that comes from within. One should be Jewish because of that special feeling that comes from the religion, the synagogue, and the community.

7. One should be Jewish because Judaism has given us a set of very useful values by which to live.

8. Being Jewish means being different. We have different beliefs and customs than other people. At the same time, it means being the same as our ancestors, carrying on our traditions and our religion, to eventually pass them on to our own children.

9. Being Jewish means acting the way that God wants His chosen people to act, and taking on the mitzvot that God commanded us to do.

10. Being Jewish means developing a deepening awareness of the spiritual possibilities that Judaism offers. It means learning to appreciate the holiness of the Sabbath and other Jewish holidays that can renew and refresh our spirit.

11. Being Jewish means family, roots, tradition, Israel, holiness, community, compassion, and justice.

Questions

1. Fill in this sentence: For me, the answer to "why be Jewish" is: _____

_____

_____

2. The reason I am less likely to follow Jewish ritual these days is: _____

_____

_____

3. How does your celebration of Judaism compare to that of your parents?

4. What are the teachings of Judaism that you are most likely going to want to impart to your children?

5. The Ethics of the Fathers says that "an ignorant person cannot be a pious person" (Pirke Avot 2:5). Do you agree or disagree with this opinion?

6. What kind of Jewish people make you feel the most proud? The least proud?

7. Share with the class a time that you encountered a Jew who made you feel uncomfortable?

8. What do you hope that the Hebrew school and Hebrew high school of the future will teach and do for your own children that you did not receive as part of your own education?

9. Describe an instance in which you were particularly aware of being Jewish.

10. What aspects of Judaism have been the most relevant to your personal life? What aspects of Judaism do you hope you might make more relevant in the years to come?

11. What do you value most about being Jewish? What does being Jewish mean to you?

12. Which of the following do you believe are essential to being a good Jew:

a. Accepting one's Jewishness and not hiding it.

b. Contributing to Jewish philanthropies.

c. Supporting Israel.

d. Supporting all human-itarian causes.

e. Belonging to a synagogue.

f. Leading an ethical life.

g. Attending worship services.

h. Observing the dietary laws.

i. Having mostly Jewish friends.

j. Marrying within the Jewish faith.

k. Believing in God.

13. Fill in the following sentence completions:

a. To me, being Jewish is _____

_____

b. If my children decided that they did not want to go to Hebrew school, I would _____

_____

c. The worst thing a Jew can do is _____

_____

d. A Jewish symbol of great importance to me is _____

_____

e. What I would need to change in order to make my life more meaningful as a Jew is _____

_____

f. My most impressive Jewish role-model is _____

_____

14. Edmond Fleg, an early-twentieth-century French author, was widely read in his day. He had left Judaism only to find it again. The following is his famous "I am a Jew" statement. Read it and decide with which parts of the statement you most agree.

> I am Jew because born of Israel and having lost it, I felt it revive within me more alive than I myself.
>
> I am a Jew because born of Israel, and having found it again, I would have it live after me more alive than it is within me.
>
> I am a Jew because the faith of Israel demands no abdication of the mind.
>
> I am a Jew because the faith of Israel asks every possible sacrifice of my soul.
>
> I am a Jew because in places where there are tears and suffering the Jew weeps.
>
> I am a Jew because in every age where the cry of despair is heard the Jew hopes.
>
> I am a Jew because the message of Israel is the most ancient and the most modern.
>
> I am a Jew because Israel's promise is a universal promise.
>
> I am a Jew because for Israel the world is not finished. Men will complete it.
>
> I am a Jew because for Israel man is not yet created. Men are creating him.
>
> I am a Jew because Israel places Man and his Unity above nations and above Israel itself.
>
> I am a Jew because above Man, image of the Divine Unity, Israel places the unity which is divine.

Fill in your own "I am a Jew Because"_____

3
Does Judaism Have Essential Principles and Values?

What is at the core of the Jewish religion? Is it ritual? Is it prayer? Is it ethics, morality, and being a good person? How would you define the so-called religious Jew? Generally speaking, people are said to be religious if they observe Jewish customs, ceremonies, and ritual.

As important as ritual observance is, however, Judaism has always held that we can most genuinely connect with God by imitating those qualities that are godly. The Book of Deuteronomy states: "Follow Adonai your God" (13:5) and "walk in all of God's ways" (11:22). What does this mean? Is it possible to follow God's presence? Rabbinic thinkers have explained that these verses teach us to follow the attributes of God. They further define these verses by telling us that the instances recorded in the Torah of God's direct contact with the patriarchs are designed to teach us how to act. One example of this is the following midrashic selection paraphrased from Genesis Rabbah 8:13:

> Just as God clothes the naked [Adam and Eve], so we should imitate God and clothe the naked; just as God visits the sick [Abraham], so should we make it our duty to visit sick people; just as God buries the dead [Moses], so must

22

we bury our dead; just as God comforts the mourners, so must we comfort those who are bereaved.

In a most beautiful talmudic teaching, the rabbis were curious to know what question God would first ask a person brought to judgment in the world-to-come. What do you think that first question might be?

Here is the teaching:

> When people are brought into judgment in the world-to-come, they are asked: "What was your occupation?"
>
> If the person answers, "I used to feed the hungry," they will say to him, "This is God's gate, you who fed the hungry may enter."
>
> . . . "I used to give water to those who were thirsty," they will say to him, "This is God's gate; you who gave water to those who were thirsty may enter."
>
> . . . "I used to clothe the naked," they will say to him, "This is God's gate, you who clothed the naked may enter."
>
> . . . and similarly with those who raised orphans, and who performed the mitzvah of tzedakah, and who performed acts of caring and lovingkindness. (Shabbat 31a)

Note that the first question asked in heaven was not "Did you believe in God?" or "Did you observe all of the rituals?" The talmudic passage clearly points to the fact it is not pure ritual but rather a person's decency that is at the very core of Judaism!

The Ethics of the Fathers, a tractate of the Talmud, speaks of three famous central principles to a Jewish life: Torah, or learning; service of God; and the performance of good deeds (Pirke Avot 1:2).

The love of learning has always dominated our faith. It is through Torah study that we learn how to lead a moral and ethical life. The Jewish people were among the first to have a system of compulsory education, and the education of the poor and those who had no parents was a communal responsibility. The ancient rabbis were truly mindful of the psychology of learning. On the first day of religious school, children were fed honey cakes in the shape of the letters of the Hebrew alphabet, so that they would associate learning with sweetness.

The second basic teaching of Judaism is service to God. From early childhood Jews are taught that God is to be worshipped out of love. Prayer is our way of pulling ourselves closer to God. And the development of congregational prayer is a distinct contribution of Judaism to the other faiths that sprang from it.

The third basic teaching of Judaism, acts of kindness, is a virtue that includes every kind of help: visiting the sick, comforting the mourner, escorting the dead to the grave. Since it consists of acts of personal kindness, it can be practiced by rich and poor alike.

Commenting on Genesis 47:29, where Jacob asks Joseph to deal kindly and truly with him after death, the Midrash Tanhuma points out that kindness shown to the dead is indeed an act of the truest love, since there is no prospect of repayment or gratitude. A poor person may one day be in a position to repay his benefactor, but a dead person cannot repay.

Comforting mourners is another example of a personal act of lovingkindness. In talmudic times it was customary to take gifts of food and especially wine to mourners to bring a little cheer into their lives. To attend a funeral is also an act of benevolence, paying the last respects to the deceased and accompanying them to their rest. Other examples of deeds of kindness include lending money to a person who is in financial difficulty, speaking a word of praise and encouragement, and being hospitable to guests.

Exercises

1. Read the following paragraph, often quoted as the biblical passage par excellence that deals with the personal act of love relating to opening one's home to a guest. After you have read the selection, answer the questions that follow:

> God appeared to Abraham by the terebinths of Mamre. He was sitting at the entrance of the tent as the day grew hot. Looking up, he saw three men standing close to him. As soon as he saw them, he ran from the entrance of the tent to greet them, and bowing to the ground, he said, "My lords, if it please you, do not go past your servant. Let a small amount of water be brought; bathe your feet and recline under the tree. And let me fetch a morsel of bread that you may refresh yourselves. Then go on, seeing that you have come your servant's way." And they replied, "Do as you have said."
>
> Abraham hastened into the tent of Sarah and said, "Quick, three measures of choice flour! Knead and make cakes." Then Abraham ran to the herd, took a calf, tender and choice, and gave it to a servant-boy, who hastened to prepare it. He took curds and milk and the calf that had been prepared, and set these things before them. And he waited on them under the tree as they ate.   (Genesis 1–8)

Questions

1. Why were the rabbis so impressed with Abraham's actions in the above selection?

2. What does this selection tell us about Abraham's personality?

3. If you had been Abraham, would you have acted similarly? Why or why not?

4. This incident took place immediately after Abraham circumcised himself. For this reason, it has been said that God was, in effect, making a personal house call to a sick person. The mitzvah of visiting the sick is called *bikkur holim* in Hebrew. Some synagogues have bikkur holim groups that visit hospitals, nursing homes, and similar institutions on a regular basis. Does your congregation have such a society? If so, what do you know about it? Perhaps you could invite a member of this group to your class to discuss its work. If your synagogue does not have one, perhaps you might like to think about a plan to start one.

5. When you are sick, what is your state of mind? What kinds of things make you feel better or help you to recover more quickly?

6. What are some of the advantages of members of a synagogue visiting fellow congregants in the hospital, even those they do not know well?

7. When guests come to your home, what do you do for them that is special? How do you make them feel comfortable and happy in your home?

Other Views of Essential Jewish Principles

Here are some sources from the Bible and the Talmud expressing the view that ethical behavior is one of God's essential demands for human beings. Read and discuss them with your teacher and classmates. Which do you feel are the most essential? Which do you feel still need to be taught and worked on?

God has told you what is good, and what God requires of you: Do justly, love mercy, and walk humbly with God. (Micah 6:8)

Love your neighbor as yourself, this is the major principle of the Torah. (Jerusalem Talmud, Nedarim 9:4)

Rabbi Yohanan ben Zakkai asked five of his students to go out and find the best attributes of a person. The following are the results: Rabbi Eliezer said, "One should have a good and kindly eye." Rabbi Joshua said: "Be a good friend." Rabbi Yossi said: "Be a good neighbor." Rabbi Simeon said: "Always try to foresee the future consequences of your actions." Rabbi Elazar said, "Have a good heart." (Pirke Avot 2:9)

Isaiah summed up the essential principles of Judaism in the following: Walk righteously. Speak honestly. Spurn profit from fraudulent dealings. Do not take a bribe. Close your ears and do not listen to malicious words. Shut your eyes against looking at evil. (Isaiah 33:15–16)

Question

What do you believe is Judaism's most essential ethical principle?

4
How Do I Make Decisions?
A Jewish Approach

When confronted with the need to make a decision or solve a problem, how do you go about doing it? What is the best way to solve a problem or evaluate an ethical situation? What course of action will you follow? How do you know what is a right or a wrong move? Listed below are some possibilities for how people make decisions. Read them and then choose those that come closest to the way you decide what to do in a particular situation.

1. I always decide to do what is best for everyone involved.
2. I always try to follow the advice of an authority (parent, teacher, rabbi).
3. I always do what makes me happiest.
4. I try to decide based upon what I believe what God would say is right.
5. I simply try to follow my own conscience.

As Jews, we are extremely fortunate to be heirs to an honorable system of ethics. The Bible and our rabbis (both modern and ancient) have written and spoken about how we ought to behave in many different types of situations. A rabbi in Ethics of the Fathers named Ben Bag Bag once said: "Turn it this way and that [i.e., the words of the Torah], for everything is in it" (Pirke Avot 5:22).

The same method can be useful when trying to solve problems. You can take a problem and consider it from one end and then the other. Problems can be broken up into smaller pieces.

Below are several additional Jewish guidelines to help you with your problem solving. After reading them you will be presented with several problems for your consideration. See if you can work with a student partner to try to solve them.

1. Judaism has always valued the principle of trying to find similar situations, precedents, examples, or guidelines from the past when dealing with a new problem. This is the way that the rabbis in the Talmud attempted to answer their questions. For example, when looking at an issue like the permissibility of a woman having an abortion, they delved into cases in the Bible and known cases in rabbinic times that related to this subject. Similarly, if you were a scientist today developing a new theory, you would want to be certain that you were aware of all of the prior theories that might shed light on the area in which you were working.

There are several ways to apply Jewish knowledge to problem solving in your life. For instance, if presented with a certain problem, you might want to research what suggestions and hints Judaism gives that may be specifically applied to it or to a similar problem. For example, let us say that you have been invited to someone's home and are beginning to eat the meal that the host has cooked just for you. You suddenly realize that the soup has a taste that is making you feel ill. What should you do? Does Judaism offer any advice regarding this problem to help you decide? In fact, there are a whole series of laws related to being a good guest which you might research, should you be presented with a similar problem in the future. For instance, we are told in chapter 6 of the Talmudic tractate of Derekh Eretz (a book dealing with proper manners) that "a good guest complies with every request that the host makes of him [her]." We are told elsewhere that "good guests leave food on their plates to show that they have been served more than enough" (Talmud, Eruvin 53b). So here are two pieces of information that you might now decide to use before continuing to eat the soup.

2. Hillel once said: "If I am not for myself, who will be for me? and if I am only for myself, what am I? And if not now, when?" (Pirke Avot 1:14). This short saying is one of the most profound in the entire Jewish tradition. While Hillel acknowledges in the first phrase of his statement the importance of an individual's (or group's) concern for self-interest, he asks in the second phrase the basic question, "If you are only interested in yourself, what kind of human being would you be?" This latter phrase is very typical of the strong interest Judaism has in the welfare of other people.

Hillel's final phrase, "if not now, when," is indicative of Judaism's view of ethics as an important part of everyday life. You simply do not just live a moral life on special occasions. Rather, as Hillel's final remark certainly suggests, a person ought to start living ethically immediately—right now! This is a very important guideline when one has to make a decision or solve a problem.

3. A third Jewish guideline for decision making would be the following: "Before judging another person, put yourself in that person's place" (Pirke Avot 2:5). Interestingly, Hillel had a hand in this piece of advice as well. Here we see that Hillel was interested in having us treat others the way we would want to be treated in a given situation. In the following story, Hillel amplifies his statement:

> One day a person came to Shammai and said, "Teach me the whole Torah while I stand on one foot and I will convert to Judaism." Shammai chased him away with the builder's rod in his hand. When be came before Hillel,

Hillel converted him and said, "What is hateful to you, do not do to your neighbor: this is the whole Torah. The rest is commentary. Now go and study."

(Talmud Shabbat 31a)

4. Follow a moderate, middle course of action is another piece of Jewish advice when it comes to solving problems. Judaism has always advocated moderation as opposed to extremism. Here is an illustrative story:

Once an important rabbi was asked how to be a good human being. He answered by telling the story of two convicts who were originally going to be executed but their sentence was reduced. They were brought to a dangerous river and a rope bridge was extended from one side to the other. Their new sentence was to cross the river using that bridge. The first managed to cross safely. The second shouted to the first, "Do you have any suggestion for how I can get across without killing myself?" The first answered, "If you find yourself leaning too far in one direction, try leaning in the other direction for balance." Thus the rabbi concluded, "If you want to be a fine human being, try not to lean too far in any direction, and if you should find a shortcoming in your personality, try to lean in the other direction to balance it."

5. Finally, Jewish tradition defines the characteristics of a wise person:

> A wise person always listens to advice.   (Proverbs 21:15)
>
> A wise person walks uprightly.   (Proverbs 15:21)
>
> A wise person learns from all people.   (Pirke Avot 4:1)
>
> The words of the wise are heard in quiet.
>   (Ecclesiastes 9:17)
>
> There are seven marks of the wise person: the wise person does not speak before one greater in wisdom, the wise person does not try to break in upon the words of his fellow, the wise person does not hasten to reply, the wise person asks what is relevant and gives a proper answer, the wise person speaks on the first point first and on the last point last.   (Pirke Avot 5:7)

Exercises

1. One of the guidelines above stated that one should try to follow a middle road when solving a problem. Can you think of a recent example where going to an extreme caused a serious problem?

2. You have just graduated as a physician and are looking for a place to live. You know that there is work to be had in the rich suburbs of your favorite city. On the other hand, you are aware of places where there is a great need for a physician but the community is poorer. How would you solve your problem using the guidelines presented above? What Jewish advice might you use?

3. You are running for student council. Your sole opponent is your best friend? How do you compete with him/her?

4. You are a football coach and your team is leading in the game by a score of 50–0. You must decide whether you wish your team to play aggressively and run up the score, or will you decide to tell your team to stop trying to score? (If you do that, you may be accused of not being fairly competitive.) What will you do? Where might you go for some Jewish advice on this issue?

5. You find a wallet in your hotel room in which there is five hundred dollars but no identification. What do you do? Where might you look for a Jewish case related to loss of money?

6. You see a fellow student (who happens to be a close friend of yours) cheating on an exam in class. You remember the biblical admonition "you shall not stand idly by when you see a wrong being perpetrated" (Leviticus 19:16) What will you do?

Unit II
People of the Covenant: Partners with God

5
Can I Doubt God's Existence and Still Be Considered Jewish?

The question of whether or not there is a God in the universe is one of the most crucial facing human beings. Beliefs related to this question have significant consequences for the meaning of human existence. Many of us are unsure of our beliefs, or don't even known whether we believe in God. Others feel that because they may have doubts or questions, they cannot sincerely involve themselves in a Jewish life to any great degree.

Can a person doubt the existence of God and still be a Jew? I believe that the answer is clearly yes! Jews throughout history have questioned God, wondering who, what, and how God is. Belief in God is not easy, and crises of faith are always to be expected. Not to have any doubts at all about God is to be religiously dead. Judaism has always stressed action over faith, and the idea that God is mostly unknowable is one of its basic ideas.

Many people have doubts about the existence of God but find that doubting God is no reason to deny Judaism as a way of life. The Jerusalem Talmud said it best when it commented, "Better that the people abandon Me [i.e., God], but still follow My laws" (Hagigah 1:7). To this the rabbis added that through living by God's laws, the people will eventually come to know God. That is to say, the more we begin to incorporate Jewish ideals into our daily routines through studying and practicing Judaism (even while having doubts about God), the more likely we may discover that God is the ultimate source of morality and ethics.

Thus, according to Judaism, one can be Jewish while having doubts and concerns about God's existence.

As students, your task is to study our faith and think about God as best you can, bearing in mind always that your ignorance of God, when compared to your knowledge, is as all the waters in the world's oceans compared with a drop of water. Ultimately you will have to make your own leap of faith regarding a belief in God. Habakkuk the prophet said that "righteous people live by their faith" (Habakkuk 2:4). Nobody can prove or disprove concerns of faith and belief, for they are personal feelings which each human being is entitled to have.

Names of God

It is quite likely that your relationship with God lies at the heart of your prayer experience. The nature of your conceptions of God will play a role in your relationship with God and the words you use to address God.

The Bible uses many different terms for God. They include "Father," "Shepherd," "King," "Judge," "Holy One," "Warrior," and "Righteous One." Did you ever wonder why there are so many different names for God? Each is intended to reveal some aspect or characteristic of God that the others do not reveal. For instance, Father and Shepherd might make you think of the qualities of tenderness or mercy. Although each name reflects a quality, God is not limited to one particular quality, nor to the sum of all of them together. Different words are used to describe God simply because the human mind needs some kind of description and everyday language must be used for that purpose.

You will now have an opportunity to learn something about your personal beliefs related to God. Three different exercises follow. You may want to choose a partner in your class and work together.

Exercise 1: Names of God

Below is a list of twenty-five different names that have been used to describe God. Read the list and share your preferences with your classmates.

1. Lord
2. God Almighty
3. Holy One
4. Shepherd
5. King
6. Our Father
7. Rock of Israel
8. The Place
9. I am that I am
10. King of Kings
11. Creator of all
12. Healer
13. The Good One
14. The Merciful One
15. The Faithful One
16. The Mighty One
17. The Redeemer
18. Lover of Israel
19. The Name
20. The Generous One
21. Hidden of Hiddens
22. Man of War
23. The Eternal One
24. God of Abraham
25. God of Jacob

Exercise 2: Faith Interview

1. How do you picture God?
2. When and in what places do you feel closest to God?
3. What are some of the doubts you have about God?
4. Has God ever answered you?
5. On what occasions do you find yourself trying most to speak with God?
6. Do you believe that God can speak to people?
7. Have you ever been upset with God? Describe such a time.
8. Do you find meaning in saying prayers to God?
9. Do you think people can train themselves to "hear" God?
10. If you were God, what things would you do differently?

Exercise 3: "I Believe" Test

In the eleventh century Moses Maimonides, a famous Jewish philosopher, wrote a creed called the Thirteen Principles of Faith. Three hundred years later, Rabbi Daniel of Rome rewrote the Thirteen Principles in poetic form. Known as the Yigdal, it is today the prayer which concludes the Friday evening Sabbath service. Some of Maimonides' principles of faith are the following:

> God is One.
> God is Eternal.
> God knows every person's thoughts.
> God gave us the Torah.
> God rewards good and punishes evil.

Here are some "I believe" statements that will help you to determine where you stand. Try to answer as many as you can, and perhaps you can discuss them with your classmates and teacher.

1. I believe that God is the Creator and Ruler of all things.
Yes _____ No _____

2. I believe that God is One and that there is no unity that is in any way like that of God.
Yes _____ No _____

3. I believe that God has no body but rather is all spirit.
Yes _____ No _____

4. I believe that God is the first and the last.
Yes _____ No _____

5. I believe that it is only proper to pray to God.
Yes _____ No _____

6. I believe that God rewards good and punishes evil.
Yes _____ No _____

7. I believe that God exists both inside and outside of people.
Yes _____ No _____

8. I believe that God knows our innermost thoughts.
Yes _____ No _____

9. I believe that God is all-powerful.
Yes _____ No _____

10. I believe that God is involved in human affairs.
Yes _____ No _____

11. I believe that God intended us never to understand certain things about the universe.
Yes _____ No _____

12. What are some other things that you believe about God?

6
Covenants and the Jewish People

A covenant is a binding agreement between two or more individuals or groups to do, or to keep from doing, some specific thing. As there are many different kinds of agreements, so too there are many different kinds of covenants. Each kind of covenant generally has its own special name. For instance, a covenant between a husband and wife is called a marriage. A covenant between a professional athlete figure and a team owner is generally called a contract. A covenant between two nations is called a treaty, while a covenant between a government and its people is called a constitution.

Here are some covenants. See if you can guess the persons and/or groups which might make them.

a. A decree   _____
b. A charter   _____
c. A will   _____
d. A guarantee   _____

Being Jewish is a matter of both choice and chance. Many of us did not choose to be Jewish. We were born of Jewish parents, raised in a Jewish home, and given a Jewish education. But the way Judaism is practiced is a matter of individual choice. Just as those who convert to Judaism are called "Jews

40

by choice," so those who are born Jewish are also in a sense Jews by choice. They can either choose to live as Jews or choose not to. The following midrash provides an illustration:

> When God decided to give the Torah, none of the nations of the world were prepared to accept it except for the people of Israel. God went to each nation in turn, but each, for some reason, refused to accept it. Finally, when God went to the Israelites, they said "na'aseh ve-nishmah"—"we will keep it and we will heed it." With these words our ancestors decided to accept the Torah's teachings and keep God's commandments. This agreement between God and the Israelites is called a *berit*—a covenant. (Mechilta de-Rabbi Ishmael, Exodus 20:2)

The Jewish people were the first to introduce the concept of a covenant between God and humankind. There are two early covenants that God made with the people of the Bible. Each had its own special sign. The first and earliest is the rainbow covenant which God made with the family of Noah after the flood when the rains had stopped (Genesis 9:9–17). In this covenant, God promised never again to destroy the entire world with a flood. The sign of this covenant was a rainbow in the sky. In return, Noah agreed to follow these seven commandments given by God to all human beings:

1. Idols must not be worshipped.
2. One should not take a false oath using the name of God.
3. Courts of law must be established.
4. One should not take the life of another person.
5. One should not commit the sin of incest.
6. One must not steal.
7. One must not eat the flesh of a living animal.

Question

Why do you think God chose the rainbow as the sign of the first covenant in the Bible? How do you feel whenever you see a rainbow? Does it remind you of this first covenant?

So important was the sign of the rainbow that the rabbis enacted a special blessing to be recited when one sees it. The blessing is:

בָּרוּךְ אַתָּה יְיָ אֱלֹהֵינוּ מֶלֶךְ הָעוֹלָם זוֹכֵר הַבְּרִית
וְנֶאֱמָן בִּבְרִיתוֹ וְקַיָּם בְּמַאֲמָרוֹ.

Barukh atah Adonai eloheinu melekh ha-olam zokher ha-berit ve-ne'eman bivrito ve-kayam be-ma'amaro.

Praised are You, Adonai our God, Sovereign of the Universe, who remembers His covenant, is faithful to it. and keeps His promise.

God also made a covenant with Abraham, promising that he would be the father of a great people and would inherit the land of Israel forever. In return, God would forever be the God of Abraham and his descendants. The sign of this covenant was circumcision.

Question

Why do you think God chose the sign of circumcision with which to enter male children into the covenant?

Today, Jewish children become Bar or Bat Mitzvah because of God's covenant with the people of Israel. The fulfillment of God's commandments (mitzvot) is the end, so to speak, of the covenant. When you became a Bar or Bat Mitzvah, assuming that you took the event seriously, you officially entered into an adult commitment with God which entails mutual responsibility. The Jewish community depends on you to be an authentic partner with God. Being God's partner means picking up where God left off. For instance, God created grain. It is people that fashion grain into bread and cake for all to enjoy. God gave us the Ten Commandments. But it takes people to transform them into living laws. When we affix a mezuzah to our doorposts, our home becomes a partner with God. When we recite the blessing over the wine at the beginning of the Sabbath, we recite "the heavens were completed, and the earth and all that is within them." When we raise the Kiddush cup and proclaim the creation, we become a partner with God. There is even a custom of holding the wine cup with one's finger pointing aloft in the shape of the Hebrew letter *shin*, which stands for Shaddai, one of God's names. This helps us to remember that our own hands can be the helping hands of God in the world.

Now it is your turn to choose. The covenant has already been made. You have become a Bar or Bat Mitzvah. For countless generations we have kept the covenant and guarded it, and tried to live by it. But it is always up to you whether Judaism will survive; and it will survive only if you continue to make Jewish choices, and make them because Judaism is important to you. In other words, continue your entire life to honor the agreement, the *berit*, between God and Israel.

Exercises

Here are some questions to help you organize your thoughts about your covenant with God.

1. The prophet Hosea defines the covenant as an act of love. between God and Israel, symbolizing their bond of partnership, which takes the form of a symbolic marriage:

> I shall betroth you to Me forever.
> I shall betroth you to Me with righteousness and justice, with love and mercy.
> I shall betroth you to Me in truth, and you shall know God. (Hosea 2:19–20)

This verse is recited when one finishes wrapping the tefillin around one's hand. In what way is our relationship to God like a marriage? What are some things we can learn from a good marriage that would better our relationship with God?

2. Abraham Joshua Heschel, a modern Jewish philosopher and teacher, wrote the following:

> There is only one way to define Jewish religion. It is the awareness of God's interest in man, the awareness of a covenant, of a responsibility that lies on Him as well as on us. Our task is to concur with His interest, to carry out His vision of our task. God is in need of many for the attainment of His ends, and religion, as Jewish tradition understands it, is a way of serving these ends, of which we are in need, even though we may not be aware of them, ends we must learn to feel the need of.
>
> Life is a partnership of God and man. . . . This is why human life is holy. God is a partner in man's struggles for justice, peace and holiness, and it is because of His being in need of man that He entered a covenant with him for all time, a mutual bond embracing God and man, a relationship to which God, not only man, is committed.[1]

[1] Heschel, A.J. *God in Search of Man* (New York: Harper and Row, 1955), pp. 241–242.

In what way is God is in need of people? In what ways has God shown the world that He is committed to the covenant?

3. The Book of Deuteronomy has an interesting and most surprising thought related to the covenant and the Jewish people:

> You are standing this day, all of you, before God . . . to enter into the covenant with Adonai your God, which God is concluding with you this day. This is so God can establish you this day as God's people and be your God as He promised and swore to your ancestors. I make this covenant with its sanctions, not with you alone, but both with those who are standing here with us this day before God, and with those who are not with us here this day.
>
> (Deuteronomy 29:9–14)

Question

What is your understanding of this ancient verse? Do you think it still applies today? Why or why not?

4. How would you define and rate our present covenant with God? Is it as strong as you would like it to be? How might you increase its strength? What mitzvot are most important to you at this point in your life, and how have they worked to help you achieve a partnership with God? What mitzvot would you like to continue to fulfill that are still not a part of your repertoire?

5. Some commentators have said that the opening statement of the Ten Commandments, "I am the God who brought you out of the land of Egypt, out of the house of bondage" (Exodus 20:2), is the opening of a treaty. It is the preamble of a treaty between God and the Jewish people. This explains why the first commandment is not phrased as a command, but rather as a statement of what God has done for the Israelites. God's accomplishments on their behalf entitle God to make demands

of them. What is your opinion of this commentary? What are some things that God has done on our behalf?

6. How does the covenant that God made with the Jewish people differ from the American Constitution? As Jews, and as Americans, why should we be bound by promises our ancestors made?

7. Write a covenant for the Jewish people for today. What would God demand of us in your covenant? What might we expect of God?

7

A Kingdom of Priests: Does God Really Play Favorites?

The Choice

The idea that the Jewish people were specially selected by God to carry out some special purpose is prominent throughout the Bible and in other Jewish teachings. The Hebrew word that usually expresses this idea is *bahar*, translated as "choose." Is it true that the Jewish people are really God's people of choice? Is it possible that God would choose to have a favorite people, namely the Jews, and give other peoples lesser roles in the divine plan for humanity? These and other questions will now be explored.

A Story: The Rabbi Questions God

The small Hassidic synagogue was crowded. It was the morning of Rosh Hashanah and all of the worshippers were immersed in their prayers. Suddenly, the voice of the rabbi rang out, "I, Levi Yitzchak, son of Sarah, speak to You, God . . ."

A strange thing indeed . . . interrupting the service. But the congregation was not at all upset. Rabbi Levi Yitzchak was often moved to speak out while people were praying. And he would often engage God in conversation.

"What is he saying?" the people asked. They leaned forward to catch his words.

"Yes, I, Levi Yitzchak, am speaking to You, God. I have a question, which is as follows: What do You, God of the world, have against the people of Israel? To whom do You always speak? To the children of Israel! To whom do You give commandments? To the children of Israel! Whom do You ask to worship You? The children of Israel! Are there no other people in the world that You can turn to? And so I ask You, what do You have against the children of Israel?"

"A good question!" answered the congregation. "Let's be quiet, for the rabbi must have an answer."

"Ah," the rabbi said. "It is because the children of Israel are dear to You!" Indeed, in the Bible do you not call them 'My children' [Ezekiel 16:21]? Well, then, blessed are You, O God."

Long afterward the people recalled that particular Rosh Hashanah day. "That was the time," they would say, "that our rabbi questioned God!"

Although not quite so dramatically as Rabbi Levi Yitzchak, many people have questioned God's relationship to the Jews. A poet once put it this way:

How odd
Of God
To choose
The Jews.

Here we see the poet calling attention to two matters. One is that God, the supposed Parent of all peoples, chose a particular people to be His own. The other is how surprising it is that God would select as the particular people the Jews.

This raises some difficult and real questions. How can the just God of the entire universe have a "favorite" people? How can this be fair to the rest of humanity? And second, why would God choose the tiny and often-persecuted group called the Jews?

How do you feel about the Jews being the chosen people? Do you feel good, or a bit uncomfortable?

What Does The Bible Say?

Several biblical passages deal with the chosen-people theme. One of the first is the mention of the Israelites as specially elected by God. God says to Abraham, "Get out of your country . . . and go into the land that I will show you, and I will make of you a great nation, and I will bless you and make your name great" (Genesis 12:1–3).

According to another story in the Bible, God chose Israel to be a special people when God led them out of Egypt and gave them the Torah on Mount Sinai.

> You have seen what I did to the Egyptians, and how I bore you on eagles' wings and brought you to Me. Now, therefore, if you will listen to Me and keep My covenant, then you shall be My own treasure from all peoples. For all the earth is Mine. And you shall be to Me a kingdom of priests and a holy nation. (Exodus 19:4–6)

Question

What do you think the preceding two passages mean? Why did God choose Abraham to be the father of the Jewish people? Why did God choose the Israelites to be a treasured nation? What was special about the Israelites that merited God's special love?

Two more passages from the Torah will illustrate God's conditions for specially choosing the Israelites as the chosen ones. The first indicates that Israel was to be God's own special vehicle for the fulfillment of certain divine purposes.

> God has chosen you to be God's treasure from all of the
> peoples that are upon the face of the earth. God did not
> set His love upon you, nor choose you, because you were
> more in number than any other people—for you were
> the fewest of all peoples—but because God loved you.
>   (Deuteronomy 7:6–8)

Because of the Jews' small numbers, any success they might
have in making God known to the world would reflect upon
the power of the idea of God. Had the Jewish nation been a
larger one with a great army, its success in making God
known would have been attributed to its might and not to
the truth of its ideas.

In a statement from the prophet Amos, we learn the following: "You alone have I singled out of all the families of the
earth. That is why I call you to account for all of your iniquities"
(Amos 3:2).

We see clearly from this that chosenness does not endow
Jews with special rights in the way that racist ideologies endow
those born into the "superior" race.

The prophet Isaiah further expands upon the concept of
chosenness:

> I am God, I have called you in righteousness . . .
> I have given you as a covenant to the people.
> For a light to the nations,
> To open the eyes that are blind.   (Isaiah 42:6–7)

Here we clearly see that according to the prophet, the Jewish
people has been assigned the mission of improving the world
and teaching other peoples to see the light. Chosenness is
thus not a privilege of which to boast but rather a task to be
undertaken. It means contributing to the betterment of the
world, what the Jewish tradition calls *tikkun olam*—"repairing
the world." It means increased responsibilities and hardship.

Many passages in the prayerbook also refer to the Jewish people as God's chosen ones. For example, the Ahavah Rabbah concludes with the words, "Praised are You, God, who has chosen your people Israel for Your service." In the first paragraph of the Aleinu, we read: "it is our duty to praise God for all. . . . God has not made us like the other nations of the world, nor has God placed us like the families of the earth. God has not made our destiny as theirs." Finally, the first blessing you recite when called to the bimah for an *aliyah* is: "Praised are You, Adonai our God, who chose us from all peoples by giving us Your Torah."

Answering The Question

Let us return to the question with which this section began.

Does God have a treasured people? Does God play favorites? Did God actually choose the Jewish people to the exclusion of others? No one really knows for sure. Some people think it is quite unlikely. But what is important is that the Jewish people *believed* that God had chosen them, and acted on that idea by accepting the covenant. And that made all the difference!

Chosenness does not mean that the Jews have been singled out for special favors. Far from it. Chosenness means being selected to carry out the special duties of being God's servant. Ours is the task of a holy people, and our mission is to remind the world that there is only One God, and that God demands righteousness and justice in the world. As God's partners, it is our task to work with God in order to bring about a just and good world.

Exercises

1. There are many different ways to consider what chosenness means today. Choose the idea below that comes closest to your own view and support your opinion by an explanation.

    a. Abandon the notion of chosenness altogether.
    b. Include all the peoples of the world under the umbrella of chosenness.
    c. Shift the burden of choosing to the people rather than making God the Chooser.
    d. See being chosen as the result of a process in which the Jewish people, searching, finds God, who is there to be found.
    e. Admit that we cannot understand everything and simply accept the concept as given by Jewish tradition.
    f. Your own definition.

I chose position _____ because:

_____

_____

_____

_____

_____

2. There was once a time when many Jews were convinced that the idea of being a chosen people was both embarrassing and outdated. How do you feel about being part of a chosen people? Do you share any of the same feelings?

3. Some prayerbooks have eliminated most if not all references to the Jews as a chosen people. How do you feel about that decision? How would you like to see the concept of chosenness handled in your own prayerbook?

4. The Jews' belief that they are the chosen people has often provoked antagonism among non-Jews. After the 1973 Yom Kippur War, Yakov Malik, the Soviet ambassador to the United Nations, said, "The Zionists have come forward with the theory of the chosen people, an absurd ideology. That is religious racism." Do you believe that anyone is still offended by the notion that the Jews are the chosen people?

5. The Yigdal prayer, which is chanted at the end of every Friday evening and holiday service, is a poetic interpretation of Maimonides' Thirteen Principles of Faith. Maimonides did not list chosenness as one of the Thirteen Principles. Can you think of any reason why it was omitted?

6. What are some ways to express the idea of chosenness in your own Jewish life?

7. David Ben-Gurion, Prime Minister of Israel, once said, "We are the chosen people only if we choose to be so." What do you think he meant by this? Do you agree with it?

8

Revelation: What Really Happened at Mount Sinai?

The Bible itself tells us how the Ten Commandments were revealed to the Jewish people. Here is a brief summary of its account:

> In the third month after the children of Israel were gone forth out of the land of Egypt, the same day they came to the wilderness of Sinai. And when they were departed from Rephidim, and came to the wilderness of Sinai, they encamped before the mount. And it came to pass, on the third day, when it was morning, that there were thunders and lightnings and a thick cloud upon the mount, and the voice of a horn exceeding loud. And all the people that were in the camp trembled. And Moses brought forth the people out of the camp to meet God. And they stood at the nether part of the mountain. . . . And God spoke all these words, saying: "I am the Lord your God, who brought you out of the land of Egypt, out of the house of bondage. . . . (Exodus 19)

The Ten Commandments follow. After the last commandment, there is this passage:

> And all the people perceived the thunderings, and the lightnings, and the voice of the horn, and the mountain smoking. And when the people saw it, they trembled

and stood afar off. And they said to Moses: "Speak with us, and we will hear. But let not God speak with us, lest we die." And Moses said to the people: "Fear not, for God is come to prove you, and that His fear may be before you, that you sin not." And the people stood afar off. But Moses drew near to the thick darkness where God was . . .   (Exodus 20)

With regard to the act of revelation, the most commonly asked questions are: What happened at Mount Sinai? How do we know that it was God speaking to Moses, and not just something Moses imagined? And even if God did in fact speak, how can we be sure that the Israelites understood it correctly. Even if God revealed His will at Mount Sinai, surely human beings throughout the generations have copied and transmitted what was said, so how can we be certain that the words we have today were God's exact words?

These are hard and difficult issues, but it is necessary to deal with them if we are going to understand the authority behind Jewish law.

Orthodox View of Revelation

There are Orthodox Jews who believe that God revealed His will at Mount Sinai both in a written and an oral form. The oral form was later written down in what is today called the Talmud, consisting of the application and interpretation of the law by rabbis who were divinely inspired. Exactly how this communication between God and the people of Israel took place is a mystery. But for the Orthodox, the fact remains that the Torah was revealed by God verbally (i.e., using words) directly to the people. Thus, God spoke words and the people directly received God's communication.

Conservative Views of Revelation

In Conservative Judaism, the nature of God's communication has been understood in various ways. For some theologians, God communicated with mortals both at Sinai and in the era of the prophets. These revelations were written down by human beings, and thus the writings included in the Bible are of diverse origins. The authority of Jewish law is based upon the fact that it is God's will, as stated first in the Torah and then by the rabbis of each generation.

Another Conservative position posits that human beings who were divinely inspired with a specific message wrote the Torah at various places and times. This position combines divine inspiration and human articulation.

In yet a third Conservative position, the Torah is understood as the human record of the encounter between God and the people of Israel. The Torah was written by human beings to whom God disclosed Himself, but without declaring specific rules or ideas. This position emphasizes the responsibility of rabbis to make appropriate changes in the tradition which accurately reflect God's will in the contemporary world.

Reconstructionist View of Revelation

Reconstructionists generally posit that human beings wrote the Torah, claiming no divinity for the product. Rabbinic authorities representing the community in each generation have an obligation to reconstruct Judaism with meaningful customs and ideas. Jewish law has authority as the folkways and customs of the Jewish people. When a particular law becomes offensive or falls into disuse, it should be changed or modified.

Reform View of Revelation

The Reform position maintains that the Torah is God's will as written by human beings. Often called "progressive revelation," this position holds that as time goes on, people will be better and better able to understand God's will. Each person must decide both what and how to obey. Each is allowed personal autonomy.

Some Final Thoughts

We do not know, nor can anyone ever know, exactly what Moses or the people at Sinai or the other prophets actually saw, heard, or felt. Many of the words used in the biblical descriptions of revelation were figurative. Prophets spoke of fire, smoke, the voice of a horn, thunder, lightning, earthquake, and even a still small voice to give us some idea of what it was like to hear God's voice. In the end, though, they could only refer to having experienced the greatness of the presence of God.

Rabbinic thinkers have had much to say about the meaning of revelation. It is your task to begin to formulate your own theological understanding of how God revealed His will to an entire people. As you continue to think about this question and challenge yourself, you will begin to develop a set of personal faith statements. This will help you to decide and define how to interpret and act upon the laws, customs, and rituals presented throughout the Bible and rabbinic Judaism.

To help you begin to organize your thoughts, we have provided some questions and exercises related to the subject of revelation.

Questions

1. Which view of revelation in this chapter do you find the most personally satisfying? The least satisfying? Why?

2. What are the unifying factors that unite all of the positions described in this chapter?

3. Do you believe that God has ever spoken or still speaks to people? What do people hear?

4. Maimonides, the medieval philosopher, wrote Thirteen Principles of Faith. One of them states, "I believe that all the words of the Torah are true." How close does this principle come to your own beliefs?

5. Do you believe that God still reveals His will to people? Has God ever revealed something to you? If so, share it with your classmates.

6. Rabbi Gunther Plaut, a Reform rabbi, has written that the Torah is "a book conjointly authored by God and by our people." Read his answer to the question "Did God really say what is in the Torah?" What is your opinion of his answer? Do any aspects of his beliefs dovetail with your own?

> Whenever we speak of who God "really" is or what God "really" does or says, we are in the realm of mystery and uncertainty. So, to answer your question, let us start with tradition . . .
>
> The idea that every word in the Torah is of divine origin was shared for thousands of years by our people and continues to be shared by Jewish and Christian orthodoxy.
>
> But over time, this concept raised difficulties. First of all, there are obvious and numerous contradictions in the Torah. Secondly, it became increasingly difficult to explain how a merciful and compassionate God could approve of slavery, order the wholesale extermination of conquered nations, make the breaking of Shabbat rules a capital offense, or be interested in the minutiae of incense burning and other aspects of the sacrificial cult.

Slowly, therefore, the idea gained ground that the Torah came into existence not in the way we had always believed but in some other fashion. Beginning in the middle of the nineteenth century, Christian scholars and progressive rabbis began to view the creation of Torah not as a one-time event that happened at Sinai, but as a long process of development which may have taken as long as eight hundred years. By and large, Liberal Jews have accepted this idea, but—and here is the most important point to remember—while it may be agreed that Torah is the result of literary and religious evolution, God did play a role in this development, but not in the way tradition had depicted it. This makes Torah a book conjointly authored by God and by our people. How is this possible?

We start with our people. They developed the concepts found in the Torah over a period of many generations. In that sense, Torah is a human document. But it is more. This tradition was handed down by pious men and women who saw themselves as servants of the Almighty—and it is my belief that in a mysterious way, God was indeed at their side, guiding their work. To me, Torah is the attempt to reach God. In this way, Torah arose from the meeting of God and God's people. Not every word in the Torah may be a witness to this meeting, but every word was meant to try and come closer to God.

There is therefore no contradiction between treating the book as a literary document on the one hand and as a religious testimony on the other. The most important thing is to approach Torah with respect, because we do not really know when God speaks. But when we study Torah we may hope that through its words the divine voice will address us.[2]

9
Mitzvot: What Does God Want from Us?

Definition

What is a mitzvah? A simple and broad definition is: anything that a Jewish person does, or refrains from doing, for a religious purpose. Defined another way, a mitzvah is a religious instruction or commandment. Although today it is often treated as a synonym for "good deed," mitzvah really refers to a specific religious obligation or sacred duty established by the rabbis many centuries ago.

Traditionally there are 613 mitzvot derived from the Torah. The mitzvot are divided into two categories: commandments between human beings and God, which might be loosely termed "ritual commandments," and commandments between human beings and one's fellow human beings, which are usually understood as "ethical commandments." Ritual commandments, such as observing the Sabbath and holy days, and keeping the dietary laws (i.e., kashrut), are intended to connect us to God. Ethical commandments, such as not murdering or not stealing, govern our relationships with other people. Some mitzvot are stated in positive language—"you shall . . ."; others in negative language—"you shall not." Christianity has no real equivalent of the Jewish concept of mitzvot. While it is true that good works are important in Christian thinking, greater emphasis is placed on faith, whereas in Judaism the fulfillment of religious acts is much more emphasized. Performing commandments is the essence of the covenant of which we spoke in Unit II of this book.

Many students who become Bar or Bat Mitzvah are required to do a mitzvah project in order to begin to experience the world of mitzvot. Do you remember your project? Bar/Bat Mitzvah is the Jewish milestone which reflects the age of legal and religious maturity, requiring performance of religious obligations. It means becoming a full member of the Jewish community with a connection to Torah, community, and God.

Traditional Judaism sees one important reason to perform commandments: God commanded them in the Torah, and rabbis throughout the ages have taught us how to perform them. In modern times, this approach makes many Jews uneasy. Those who have doubts about God are not likely to abide by laws presented as the commands of a deity in whom they do not believe. Those who do believe in God are often not satisfied with the tradition's insistence that God demands obedience, because that takes away their right to decide what to do and their ability to make personal decisions.

Of course there are many other reasons to perform mitzvot. Read the following reasons and choose the ones that come closest to your reason for fulfilling mitzvot:

a. Doing mitzvot helps me to feel more Jewish and help to develop my Jewish identity.

b. Doing mitzvot that relate to ethics will help me to improve the world.

c. Doing mitzvot helps to connect me with God. It's part of the covenantal relationship that we have established with God.

d. Doing mitzvot helps to connect me to the Jewish people past, present, and future.

e.   Doing mitzvot helps to make my life more holy, adding sanctity to it.

f.   Doing mitzvot helps to train me in developing beliefs and defining my faith.

g.   Doing mitzvot helps to enhance God's reputation and honor.

h.   Doing mitzvot helps to establish Israel's national identity.

i.   I do mitzvot because they reflect the will of God, and it is my duty to carry them out.

j.   For doing a mitzvah I will be rewarded by God.

Things You Should Know About Mitzvot

There are several important ideas to remember whenever you think about a mitzvah. The first is that many scholars throughout the ages have tried to figure out why the various mitzvot were commanded in the first place. No one has a true handle on the reasons the commandments are to be performed. You are entitled to develop your own opinion about their various rationales. Here are some other thoughts and ideas related to mitzvot for your consideration:

Mitzvot are meant to be performed with proper intention and attitude (in Hebrew, *kavvanah*). This is generally understood to mean thinking about the source of the mitzvah (i.e., God) and the purpose, which is to make ourselves holy by performing it.

Some commandments are time-related, others are non-time-related. Time-related ones are those which must be observed at a particular time each day and not whenever you feel like it. Examples of time-related mitzvot are reciting the Shema prayer, putting on tallit and tefillin, and eating matzah during Passover. Non-time-related ones include the commandments related to helping the poor, caring for animals, and giving tzedakah. These can be done at any time.

The mitzvot are categorized as "light" (less important) and "heavy" or "serious" (more important). This distinction was made by several rabbinic authorities. Maimonides classified the act of celebrating a festival as a light mitzvah and the mitzvah of learning Hebrew as a more serious commandment.

There are rational and nonrational mitzvot. Not all commandments are designed for our minds. Many are intended for our souls. The rabbis distinguished between commandments which they regarded as rational and others which appeared less logical. Ethical commandments, such as do not steal or kill, are rational commandments. They are rational because the reason for them is self-evident. Keeping kosher is an example of a nonrational commandment. The reasons for nonrational commandments are not self-evident; in effect, they are commandments because they were commanded.

There are seven commandments that are not based on verses in the Torah. These are called rabbinic mitzvot (in Hebrew, *mitzvot de-rabbanan*) because they were added by the rabbis. These include: washing one's hands before eating, lighting Sabbath candles, reciting the Hallel psalms, lighting Hanukkah candles, reading the scroll of Esther at Purim, and reciting a blessing when you enjoy something like eating cake.

The rabbis used the Hebrew phrase *simhah shel mitzvah* ("the joy of doing a commandment") to express the happiness that one ought to feel every time one performs a mitzvah.

The rabbis used the phrase *hiddur mitzvah* ("beautifying the commandment") as a way of telling us that we should try to enhance the performance of a commandment by beautifying it. Thus, when you build a sukkah for the holiday of Sukkot, you should decorate it as beautifully as possible. This not only enhances the mitzvah but adds to the glory of God.

The rabbis used the term *hivvuv mitzvah* ("love of the mitzvah") to refer to the appropriate attitude when performing a commandment. Mitzvot are to be performed with abounding love, beauty, and dignity. The example often given with regard to this concept is the person who in buying something to perform a particular commandment does not bargain over the price, but pays at once whatever is asked. This is done to show that love of God is greater than attachment to material goods.

The term *zerizut* means "alertness." According to the rabbis, one's attitude toward performing a commandment is indicated by the alertness one exhibits when the time comes for its performance. As the psalmist said, "I have hastened and not delayed in the observance of Your commandments" (Psalms 119:60). Thus a mitzvah which can be performed at any time of the day should be carried out as early as possible. That is why it is meritorious for a *berit milah* (circumcision) to be performed in the morning rather than in the afternoon, because one should always hasten to perform commandments.

The term *bizui mitzvah* refers to treating a commandment disrespectfully. Using a sacred object for a secular purpose is disrespectful. For instance, it is expressly forbidden to count money by the light of the candles in a hanukkiah, for this shows great disrespect for the mitzvah. One must also take care not to be disrespectful toward objects with which a mitzvah was been performed, such as old tzitzit or tefillin. These must be not thrown away but buried in the ground in order to prevent their desecration.

The term *lishmah* means "for its own sake." This refers to the rabbinic dictum that mitzvot ought to be performed without any ulterior motive or expectation of a reward.

The mitzvot have been classified into those between oneself and other people (*mitzvot bein adam le-haveiro*) and those between oneself and God (*mitzvot bein adam le-makom*). Mitzvot between a person and God include the act of eating in a sukkah on Sukkot and observing Shabbat. Mitzvot between people include helping one another in time of distress and returning lost objects.

Responsibility: It's Up To You

Preparing to become a Bar or Bat Mitzvah is not an easy task. There were additional lessons to learn the musical notations for Haftarah and Torah reading, and many of you were probably involved in doing a mitzvah project where you had an opportunity to perform and document your fulfillment of mitzvot. The commitment to the continued performance of mitzvot after becoming Bar/Bat Mitzvah is totally up to you. With so many to perform and so many other choices to make in life, this is not a simple task. All too often Jewish teenagers have sought to escape from the new responsibility imposed upon them. Throughout history our people have cried out against one or another of the Torah's requirements, its many disciplines and restraints.

Moses himself anticipated this reaction some thirty-two hundred years ago, when, in his final message to the people, he pleaded with them:

> Surely this teaching, which I enjoin upon you this day, is not too hard for you, neither is it beyond reach. It is not in the heavens, that you should say, "Who among us can go up to the heavens and bring it to us, and impart it to us, that we may observe it?" Neither is it beyond the sea, that you should say, "Who among us can cross to the other side of the sea, and bring it to us, and impart it to us that we may observe it?" No, the thing is very close to you in your mouth and in your heart, to observe it.
>
> (Deuteronomy 30:14)

In other words, Moses was telling his people, "It's up to you!" Given the desire and faith to do it, it can be done. Moses' last words are as relevant today as they were centuries ago when they were first uttered.

Rabbi Jeffrey Salkin, in his book *Being God's Partner*, defines partnership with God as "picking up where God left off." For instance, when we say the blessing over bread, we bring God's work to perfection by showing our appreciation for the wheat which God created. When we pray for peace, singing prayers like Oseh Shalom, we become God's partner by pro-actively working in our own lives to bring peace to our community and our world. When we praise God in the morning for clothing the naked, we become God's true partner by bringing clothes to a local clothing bank for distribution to those in need.

Bar/Bat Mitzvah is not something you just have; it is something you become, if you choose to. We all have freedom of choice to decide how Judaism and its mitzvot will play in our living of life itself.

When God was about to hand the reins of leadership over to Joshua, successor of Moses, he gave him this charge: "Be strong and of good courage." May you use your wisdom while doing mitzvot and always be concerned for the sanctity of people, time, and place.

Questions

1. Define the words "responsibility" and "privilege." Becoming a Bar/Bat Mitzvah involves both responsibility and privilege. What are some of the responsibilities that you now have as B'nai and B'not Mitzvah? What are the privileges that you enjoy?

2. The rabbis wrote that "the reward of a mitzvah is another mitzvah" (Pirkei Avot 4:2). Do you agree? Is there any truth to it as it relates to your own performance of commandments?

3. Hillel was once asked which mitzvah he considered the most important. He replied, "What is hateful to you, do not do to others" (Talmud Shabbat 31a). Rabbi Akiva said, "Love your neighbor as yourself" (Sifra 89b). If you were to choose one mitzvah as the most important of them all, which would you choose and why?

4. Why do you perform mitzvot? How do you decide which ones to perform? Share your reasons with your classmates.

5. Are there any mitzvot that you do even though you do not have a personal rationale for doing them?

6. The Talmud states, "Greater is one who is commanded to do something and does it, than one who is not commanded to do something and does it" (Kiddushin 31a). What does this statement mean, and do you agree with it?

7. The Talmud informs us that "a person should always occupy himself with Torah and the commandments, even if not for their own sake, for even if one does them with an ulterior motive, one will eventually come to do them for their own sake" (Pesahim 50b). How do you feel about this statement?

8. Of the 613 mitzvot, approximately forty deal with feelings. An example of a mitzvah that deals with a feeling is "Do not be jealous of your neighbor's possessions" (Exodus 20:14) .

Another example is "Love your neighbor as yourself" (Leviticus 19:18). Is it possible to feel a certain way simply because you are commanded to feel that way? Is it difficult to perform mitzvot that deal with feelings?

9. Think of some specific examples in your life in which observing commandments would help you to be part of what a holy people is supposed to be.

10. The second paragraph of the Shema states the following: "If you will earnestly heed the mitzvot I give you, to love God with all of your heart and soul . . . then I will favor your land with rain at the proper season. . . . Take care lest you be tempted to forsake God and turn to false gods to worship. For then the wrath of God will be directed against you, and God will close the heavens and hold back the rain." Explain this verse. Do you believe that God will reward you for following the mitzvot?

11. Exodus 19:5–6 states: "If you will obey Me faithfully and keep My covenant, you shall be My treasured possession among all the peoples. Indeed, all the earth is Mine, but you shall be to Me a kingdom of priests and a holy nation." In what way will keeping God's mitzvot help us to become a holy people? How do you understand the concept of "holy"? Do we as a people remain holy no matter what we do? Why would the prospect of gaining the status of God's "treasured possession" motivate us to obey God's laws?

12. Give some examples from your own life where following the commandments identified you as a Jew, either in your own mind or in the eyes of others.

13. Which mitzvot do you most enjoy doing? Give some examples of those that you least enjoy doing, but continue to do anyway.

14. Of all the different reasons for obeying Jewish law and performing mitzvot, which are the most persuasive to you? Why?

15. Give some examples of commandments between a person and God and those between a person and a fellow human being. Use the space below to list them. You may also wish to choose a partner and share your list and thoughts concerning them.

Which do you follow? Which do you not yet follow? Which do you find most difficult to follow?

Mitzvot Between God and People

1._____

2._____

3._____

4._____

Mitzvot Between People and People

1._____

2._____

3._____

4._____

10
Isn't It Enough to Be Ethical?
The Challenge of Ritual

The Hebrew language has no precise term for the word "ritual." The many ritual observances in Judaism are more likely to be referred to as traditions, customs, or even mitzvot. Ritual plays an important part in everyone's life. Understood in general parlance as any formal and customarily repeated act or series of acts or habits, rituals clearly are a part of the fabric of our lives. Think about what you do when you go to sleep or awaken in the morning. Think about the seat you take in your local synagogue, or your normal routine on any given day of the week, and you are likely to have established a rather predictable routine. Indeed, establishing a comfortable routine is a necessity of life. It helps to provide us with order and stability.

Judaism has a great many rituals. Examples include the dietary laws, keeping the laws of the Sabbath and the holidays, wearing tallit and tefillin, praying every day, and so on. These rituals are mitzvot, but for many modern Jews they do not seem nearly as obligatory as the mitzvot that deal with ethics and morality. Many Jews wonder whether it isn't enough simply to behave in an ethical manner. Commandments that have a clear moral force about them are more likely to be observed because people see them as helping to remind us of what is right and good in the eyes of God. In light of this, our rabbinic thinkers have often attempted to search for the underlying moral and symbolic value of the many rituals that on the surface appear to have little or no moral basis.

The Prophets and Ritual

The biblical prophets assigned a clear priority to the ethical commandments over the ritual. Here are three examples of what they had to say about ritual. After you read them, ask yourself what it is, according to the prophets, that God wants from the Jewish people.

> Your new moons and fixed holidays fill Me with hate. They are a burden to Me. I cannot endure them. . . . Wash yourselves clean. Put your evil doings away from Me. Learn to do good. Devote yourselves to justice. Help people that were wronged. Uphold the rights of the orphan. Defend the widow.   (Isaiah 1:14–17)

> With what shall I approach God . . . with burnt offerings and a calf a year old? Would God be pleased with a thousand rams or streams of oil? Shall I give my firstborn for my sins? . . . God has told you what is good and what God requires of you: Only to do justly and to love goodness and to walk modestly with Him.   (Micah 6:6–8)

> I hate your festivals. I am not satisfied with your celebration of holy days. Spare me the sound of your prayers.   (Amos 5:21–22)

Questions

1. According to the prophets, what was the problem with the ritual sacrifices offered by the Jewish people?

2. How might what they said relate to our own prayers and rituals? What are Isaiah and Micah telling us about the role and function of the modern-day synagogue? What do you think American Jews would do if some respected rabbis were suddenly to issue a public statement saying that praying in synagogues was not what God wanted and that God hated it?

What Were the Prophets Saying?

Were the prophets really against ritual? Yes, if the ritual was only an end unto itself. In championing the importance of ethics, the prophets were not averse to ritual and ceremony. What they were condemning and chastising was adherence to the form of the ritual while violating the spirit and true intent behind it. Thus, the prophets said that both they and God abhorred the Sabbath and festivals and Israel's sacrifices when these were accompanied by flagrant violations of God's moral laws. Above all, they wanted the people to be concerned with the oppressed and disadvantaged, with justice and compassion.

In the eyes of the prophets, the ritual had become rote and mechanical; it was not leading to the ultimate goal, which was serving God and our fellow human beings. When the ritual was carried out in the proper spirit, the sacrificial animals would be seen only as a means to a great end. They were meant to remind the people of their ultimate mission, namely, to conduct themselves ethically and help to repair the problems of the world.

The Real Role of Ritual

It is clear from the prophets that justice and righteousness is God's supreme demand. God ridicules the religious hypocrisy of those who carefully observe Judaism's rituals but ignore its ethics. Does this mean that God does not want us to perform rituals at all? What then is the role of ritual?

We must remember the context in which the prophets spoke. They were talking to people who brought the right sacrifices but then cheated their fellow human beings.

In Jewish tradition, ritual and ethical mitzvot are treated as equivalent. God wants both, but God wants the ritual commandments to help raise our the level of our ethical consciousness.

Rabbi David Wolpe has said that Jewish ritual is the discipline of pause and focus. For instance, the observance of the weekly Sabbath ritual and rest helps us to pause and reflect upon the meaning of our lives and the role of God in the universe. Saying a blessing over bread helps us to appreciate the fact that we have food to eat and that a Creator is the source of our food. It may also help to arouse our awareness of others who do not have enough to eat and spur us to help the hungry.

Fasting on Yom Kippur can remind us of all of the hungry people throughout the country and the world whose fast every day is involuntary. Our fast could lead us to a desire to help the hungry. God wants us to remind ourselves through ritual of our partnership with Him so that by serving God we can serve others. Performing ritual is a means to that end. To do it takes discipline and commitment.

The great sage Hillel once said: "If I am not for myself, who will be for me. And if I am only for myself, what am I? And if not now, when?" (Pirke Avot 1:14).

Questions

1. Review the rituals listed below. Some of them you probably already perform. How can doing them help to raise your ethical consciousness?

   a. Saying Kiddush over wine.
   b. Washing your hands and reciting a berakhah before a meal.
   c. Wearing a tallit.
   d. Wearing a kippah.
   e. Eating matzah on Passover.
   f. Affixing a mezuzah to your doorpost.
   g. Lighting a hanukkiah.
   h. Keeping kosher.

2. What are some Jewish ritual acts that have helped to make you a better person?

3. Prayer is an important ritual in Judaism. It is subject to rigorous discipline, including where, when, and in what company we must pray. When do you find yourself praying to God? What prayers in the siddur are the most meaningful to you?

4. Some people rarely pray in the synagogue, but when they lose a loved one, they make it their business to attend daily services and recite the Mourner's Kaddish. Why do you think this is so? What does it tell you about this particular Jewish ritual?

5. Is there anything that rabbis could do with regard to prayer services that might encourage more young people to attend?

6. Which Jewish ritual have you found especially meaningful in recent years?

7. Which Jewish rituals do you have the most difficulty understanding?

8. Here is a story about prayer. Read it and see if you can draw some conclusions.

> Once there was a simple shepherd who was very ignorant and did not even know how to pray. But he wanted to pray, and so he created his own prayer. Every morning he would say, "God of the World, You know that I am a shepherd, and the people pay me for taking care of sheep. But if You had sheep and gave them to me to herd for You, I would take nothing from You, because I love You."
>
> Once a learned man met the shepherd and heard him praying, and was shocked. "Don't pray that way," he said. The learned man taught the shepherd the blessings, the Shema, and the Amidah in the proper order, and made him promise that he would not pray as he did before.
>
> But when the learned man went away, the shepherd forgot the formal prayers, and since he was now afraid to recite his own prayer, he did not pray at all.
>
> But the learned man had a dream, and in it he heard a voice saying: "Why have you robbed Me? Tell him to pray as he always did."
>
> At once the learned man went to the shepherd and said: "Say what you used to say, for God desires only the heart." (Yehudah HeHassid, Sefer Hassidim)

Unit III
Between People: Why Be Good?

11
What Is Ethics?

There is no question but that Judaism wants us to be ethical people.[2] In fact, according to Isaiah 1 and Hosea 6:6, and most of the literature of the prophets, God wants us to be ethical and good people.

What exactly does the word "ethics" mean? One definition is that it involves the study of moral problems. Some questions commonly asked when confronting ethical moral issues are:

> How do you know when something is right or wrong?
> Is it "good" or "bad"?
> Why be "good"?
> Am I dealing fairly with someone else?
> Which is more important—the individual or the group?

It is not easy to make moral decisions. As societal values continue to change, decisions of good or bad, right or wrong, grow more difficult.

Rabbi Sidney Greenberg, in his book *Say Yes to Life*, presents four sets of questions to assist us in making ethical decisions:

[2]My thanks to the United Synagogue Department of Youth Activities for permission to use excerpts from chapters 2, 4, 6 and 9 in my *Derech Eretz: The Path to an Ethical Life* (New York: United Synagogue of Conservative Judaism Department of Youth Activities, 1995).

1. Can the decision I make stand the glare of publicity? What if everybody knew about it? Does it need a cover-up? Could I tell my parent or my child what I did?

2. Will my best self approve the action I am contemplating? Does it satisfy my own highest standards of behavior? Is it compatible with my conscience? Will it leave me with guilt or with pride?

3. Where does this action lead? What are its likely results?

4. What if everybody did what I am contemplating? What kind of society would we fashion? Would the world be a better or a shabbier place to live in if my action became the accepted norm, the universal guide?[3]

These are important questions worth thinking about when you need to make an ethical decision.

Ethics in the Bible and Rabbinic Thoughts

There is no comprehensive concept in the Bible which parallels the modern concept of ethics. The Hebrew term *musar* took on the meaning of "ethics" in later Hebrew, but in the Bible it merely indicates the educational function fulfilled by the father: "Hear, my son, the instruction of your father" (Proverbs 1:8). In the Bible, ethical demands are considered an essential part of the demand that God places upon human beings. And in Judaism, it is the concept of the human being created in God's image which forms the foundation of ethics.

Indeed, wherever something is left to a person's conscience, the Torah adds the words "You shall revere God" or "I am God." For example, Leviticus 19:3 says that we must shall fear our mother and father, and keep God's Sabbath: "I am God." Other examples include leaving a corner of one's field for a poor person, not being a talebearer, and not hating

[3]Greenberg, *Say Yes to Life* (New York: Crown, 1982), pp. 42–43.

one's neighbor. All of these laws are followed by the phrase "I am God." Thus, the foundation of biblical ethics includes the belief that every human being is created in the image of God and is therefore entitled to respect.

In the Bible, the root *tzedek*, meaning "righteousness," occurs some five hundred times in all of its inflections. Thus, doing what is right and just is the essence of biblical ethics. The person who refrains from wrongdoing and makes an effort to establish what is right is called a righteous person.

For rabbinic thinkers, too, the ethical ideal was the tzaddik, the righteous and good person. According to the Talmud, one single righteous person can ensure the very existence of the world (Yoma 38b).

The Book of Deuteronomy states: "Follow Adonai your God" (13:5) and "walk in all of God's ways" (11:22). What do you think this means? Is it possible to follow God's presence? The rabbis explain that these verses are intended to teach us that we should follow God's *attributes*. They cite the instances in the Torah of God's direct contact with the patriarchs, designed to teach us how to act. One example is the following midrash:

> Just as God clothes the naked [Adam and Eve], so should we clothe the naked; just as God visits the sick [Abraham], so should we make it our duty to visit sick people; just as God buries the dead [Moses], so must we bury our dead; just as God comforts the mourners, so must we comfort those who mourn.   (Genesis Rabbah 8:13)

Avoiding Evil

The command to refrain from hurting others and to avoid doing evil to the weak and oppressed is fundamental to biblical ethics, and most of the ethical mitzvot belong to this category:

Social Justice
You must not carry false rumors, nor join hands with the guilty to act as a malicious witness. You should not side with the mighty to do wrong . . . nor shall you show deference to a poor person in a dispute. (Exodus 23:1–2)

Avoidance of Bribery
Do not take bribes, for bribes blind the clear-sighted.
(Exodus 23:8)

Avoidance of Robbery and Oppression
You shall not wrong a stranger or oppress him.
(Exodus 22:20, Deuteronomy 24:14)

The Prohibition of Gossip
You shall not go up and down as talebearer among your people.   (Leviticus 19:16)

Demands to Sustain the Poor
If there is a needy person among you, one of your kinsmen in any of your settlements in the land that God is giving you, do not harden your heart and shut your hand against your needy kinsman.   (Deuteronomy 15:7–11)

Returning Lost Property
When you encounter your enemy's ox or donkey wandering, you must return it to him.   (Exodus 23:4)

Biblical ethics reach their highest level with the commandment: "You shall not hate your fellow person in your heart," which concludes with "love your neighbor as yourself" (Leviticus 19:17–18).

Finally, the general trend of social ethics was summed up by the prophet Micah, who wrote, "God has told you what is good, and what is required of you: do justice, love mercy, and walk humbly with your God" (Micah 6:8).

The Medieval Musar Movement

In the Middle Ages, the Hebrew term *musar* gradually acquired the connotation of moral principles which tend to improve human relationships. Teachers and preachers of musar attempted to educate people toward strict ethical behavior. The musar movement soon developed its own special literature. One of its outstanding works was the *Sefer Hassidim* by Rabbi Yehudah the Hassid (1150–1217). The *Sefer Hassidim* expounds a variety of ethical principles, including the following:

Do not purposely mislead anyone. Do not say that a certain price has been offered for your merchandise if that is not true. Call the attention of a non-Jew to an error he has made in overpaying you, for it is better that you live on charity than that you disgrace the Jewish name by cheating. If a murderer seeks refuge with you, give him no place to dwell, even if he is a Jew. If you are in debt, pay your debts before you contribute to charity.

The Ideal Ethical Person

The Jewish ideal is not only to behave ethically, but to have an ethical character. The Torah teaches us not only to act and behave well but also to become good persons and good Jews. The task of the good Jew is to strive to be an even better Jew. There is no rest for righteous people. A good person must always strive to do better and be proactive, so as to make further progress toward the ultimate goal, the perfecting of the world.

The Ethics of the Fathers sums up the ideal ethical character in this way:

> Whoever has these three attributes is of the disciples of Abraham our ancestor, but whosoever has three other attributes is of the disciples of the wicked Balaam. A good eye, a humble mind, and a lowly spirit are the marks of Abraham our father. An evil eye, a haughty mind, and a proud spirit are the marks of the disciples of Balaam the wicked. . . . The disciples of Abraham enjoy this world and will inherit the world-to-come.   (Pirke Avot 5:19)

Exercises

Here are some examples of the types of questions that can be raised when discussing ethical issues. To make these questions come alive, you may wish to divide into small groups and role-play each of the three situations.

1. How do you compete for a position on your school basketball team when your best friend is your main competitor?
2. You are in the same math class as the kid who lives next-door. You are taking an exam and see him cheating. What do you do?
3. You have a problem to solve related to a family relationship. Your mother and your father give you different pieces of advice. What do you do?

After completing each of the role-playing situations, you may wish to discuss the basis for the decisions you ultimately made. Would your solutions to these dilemmas always be the same?

Derekh Eretz And Ethics

The Hebrew term *derekh eretz* literally means "the way of the land," but efforts to define it in English have utilized such concepts as decency, proper decorum, etiquette, proper manners, common courtesy, and savoir faire. Because derekh eretz designates the way a Jew ought to behave, it clearly has ethical implications, referring to a code of good and proper behavior.

Rabbinic literature is replete with rules of dignified conduct and common courtesy, covering such areas as proper speech, proper dress, how to eat and drink, treatment of others, and one's personal relations. Two talmudic tractates, Derekh Eretz

Rabbah and Derekh Eretz Zutah, contain a collection of ethical teachings related to rules of conduct and proper behavior.

Exercises

Here is a small cross-section of rules of conduct, listed by category. Read them and then try to find their rationale.

Communication

Why was Gehazi punished? Because he called his teacher by name.   (Talmud Sanhedrin 100a)

Never use an indecent expression, even if you have to use more words to complete the sentence.
                                   (Talmud Pesahim 3a)

Accustom your tongue to say "I do not know." lest you be led to falsehood and be apprehended.
                                   (Derekh Eretz Zutah, chap. 3)

Overlook an insult and do not glorify yourself by your fellow person's humiliation.
                                   (Derekh Eretz Zutah, chap. 6)

Refrain from making complaints, because if you complain against others you will be led to further sin.
                                   (Derekh Eretz Zutah, chap. 9)

Teacher-Student Relations

A student should visit his teacher every holiday.
                                   (Talmud Rosh Hashanah 16b)

Never leave the company of a teacher or even of your fellow unless you have previously obtained that person's consent. (Derekh Eretz Rabbah, chap. 5)

Visiting and Being a Guest
The answer "yes" [to a knock on the door] does not mean "enter" but "wait." (Talmud Bava Kamma 33a)

Always be pleasant upon entering and leaving a house. (Derekh Eretz Rabbah, chap. 4)

Do not sit down at a table to eat before your elders have taken their seats. (Derekh Eretz Zutah, chap. 6)

Study of Torah Combined with Ethics
Rabbi Elazar ben Azariah said, "If there is no Torah, there is no derekh eretz. And if there is no derekh eretz, there is no Torah." (Pirke Avot 3:23)

Rabban Gamliel, the son of Rabbi Judah the Prince, said, "The study of Torah is good together with derekh eretz, since the effort of both of them makes one forget sin." (Pirke Avot 2:2)

Questions

1. What do you think the rabbis meant when they wrote in Ethics of the Fathers, "If there is no derekh eretz, there is no Torah, and if there is no Torah, there is no derekh eretz"?

2. What are some common courtesies that teachers ought to extend to students? What are some courtesies that students ought to extend to teachers? Do you find that teachers and students extend courtesies to each other?

3. Is it disrespectful to call a teacher by his/her first name?

4. Telling the truth is an essential belief in Judaism and virtue in Jewish ethical conduct. Read the following talmudic

passage. It deals with the value of telling the truth in consonance with derekh eretz. The story relates to whether or not a person ought to compliment a bride even if she is not particularly beautiful. Here is the story:

> Our rabbis taught, "How does one dance before the bride?" Bet Shammai says, "A bride as she is." Bet Hillel says, "A beautiful and gracious bride." Bet Shammai then said to Bet Hillel, "If she were lame or blind, would you still say to her, 'A beautiful and graceful bride,' since the Torah says, 'Keep far from falsehood' [Exodus 23:7]?" Bet Hillel said to Be Shammai, "According to you, if someone made a bad purchase in the market, should you praise it before him or defame it? Surely you should praise it." Therefore the sages concluded: One should always be pleasant toward people.   (Ketubbot 16b–17a)

Questions

1. How does this story relate to the theme of derekh eretz?

2. Do you agree with the conclusion of the rabbis?

3. Do you offer compliments even if they are not totally deserved?

How Should A Person Behave?
Why Be Good?

The foundation of Jewish ethics is the belief that every human is created in the image of God. The word "image" does not imply a physical representation, but a spiritual one. We are taught that human beings possess qualities which are godlike in essence that set them aside from the animal kingdom. In the social dimension this translates to mean that people have a responsibility to behave toward each other with dignity and goodness, and to act in a moral manner that befits the divine holiness that is an essential part of their nature.

Judaism has always portrayed human beings as possessing two basic inclinations—the good impulse (*yetzer tov*) and the evil impulse (*yetzer ra*). These two impulses are constantly wrestling within our souls, struggling to overcome each other.

Jewishly speaking, a good and ethical person is not simply someone who does not cause harm or evil to others. To be an ethical person by Jewish standards means more than simply not hurting others. It means being a person who actively pursues the good in life. Let me cite a couple of examples.

It is not enough to simply refrain from hurting others. One must, on the contrary, get involved when one sees a wrong being committed. The Torah says: "Do not stand idly by on the blood of your neighbor" (Leviticus 19:16).

Similarly, it is not enough to merely refrain from doing unjust things. To be a good and ethical person, one must actively seek out and try to correct a wrong done by another: "Justice, justice, shall you pursue" (Deuteronomy 16:20), and "you shall burn the evil from out of your midst" (Deuteronomy 17:7).

The first Israelite to set an example in the area of being a good person was Abraham. When he learned that God was about to destroy all of the people of Sodom and Gomorrah, Abraham challenged God's justice, bargaining with God to find enough good people for the sake of whom God would spare the two cities. The Book of Esther records that when Mordecai overheard two men in the court of King Ahasuerus plotting to kill him, he was proactive, reporting the incident to his cousin Queen Esther, and the king's life was ultimately saved.

Being good and behaving ethically means acting and responding to anything that is wrong in the world. It means being the keepers of our brothers and sisters, actively seeking out wrongs and trying to correct them.

Questions

1. Can you think of times when the so-called evil impulse tried to get the best of you? How were you able to overcome it?

2. The Yiddish word *mensch* designates a person who is good and who loves, respects, and is always totally devoted to others. A mensch is kind, humble, reliable, honest, unselfish, and compassionate. Who were some of the mensches who have played a part in your life?

3. There have been many reported incidents of gangs beating someone up while other people looked on, remaining uninvolved. Why do you think so many people choose not to get involved when they see an evil being perpetrated? What can we do to change their mindsets?

4. Describe your ideal ethical person:

_____

_____

_____

_____

_____

12

The Ethics of Speech and Communication

Usually when we think of ethics we think in terms of our actions toward other people, whether right or wrong. Yet ethical issues can also extend into the realm of communication and speech—the way in which we use words both orally and in written form. The following midrash teaches us an important lesson about the power of the tongue:

> One of the rabbis sent his servant to the market with the general instruction: "Buy the best thing you can find there." The servant returned with a tongue. Later, the rabbi asked him to go back to the market to buy the worst thing one could find. The servant again came back with a tongue. "What's with you?" asked the rabbi. "Here, I have asked you to buy both the best and the worst, and you come back with a couple of tongues." "That's true," responded the servant. "After all, is not a good tongue one of the best things in the world and an evil tongue one of the worst?" (Leviticus Rabbah, 33)

Words can be extremely potent weapons. When used correctly and appropriately, they can soothe and comfort. When used improperly, they can hurt, injure, and curse. The Hebrew for "words" is *devarim*. With a slight change in vowels, it becomes *devorim*—bees that sting. The power of words is described in the Bible as follows: "Death and life are in the power of the tongue" (Proverbs 18:21).

What are words able to do that is unethical? Look at the ninth of the Ten Commandments and you will see the harm that words can cause: "You shall not bear false testimony against your neighbor" (Exodus 20:13). This commandment is meant to remind us that someone who is giving testimony against a neighbor ought to be very careful. False testimony can ruin a person's reputation.

Biblical Ethics of Communication

Here are some verses related to the power of the tongue as manifested in the Bible.

> There are those who speak like the piercings of a sword. But the tongue of the wise is health.   (Proverbs 12:18)

> A lying tongue hates those who are hurt by it. And a flattering mouth works ruin.   (Proverbs 26:28)

> The words of a talebearer are as wounds, and they go down into the innermost parts of the belly.(Proverbs 18:8)

> A soft answer turns away anger, but grievous words stir up anger.   (Proverbs 15:1)

> Do you see a person that is hasty in his words? There is more hope for a fool than for him.   (Proverbs 29:20)

The Ethics of Communication in Rabbinic Writings

There are many rules concerning speech and the primary role it plays in our lives. A Jew is forbidden to insult, shame, embarrass, defame, slander, curse, or swear falsely. Rabbi Israel Meir Hakohen Kagen, toward the end of the nineteenth century, wrote a book outlining the seriousness of the sin of gossip. In accordance with an old custom, he is often referred to by its title, *Hafetz Hayyim*, which was drawn from the biblical verse "Who is the person that desires life, loves days, that he may see good therein? Then keep your tongue from evil, and your lips from speaking guile" (Psalms 34:13–14).

Exercises

Read the following Hassidic story and see if you can discern its moral.

> A man would often slander his rabbi until one day, feeling remorseful, he begged for forgiveness and indicated that he was willing to undergo any penance to make amends. The rabbi told him to take several pillows from his home, cut them open, and scatter the feathers to the winds. The man did so immediately, and returned to the rabbi to notify him that he had fulfilled his request. The rabbi then told him, "Go and gather all the feathers that the wind has scattered. For though you are sincerely remorseful and truly desirous of correcting the evil which you have done, it is about as possible to repair the damage done by your words as it will be to recover the feathers."
>
> (Hassidic folktale)

Here are some additional rabbinic saying related to the use and misuse of words:

Whoever dirties one's mouth, even though it had been decreed in heaven that he should live seventy years, causes the decree to be reversed.   (Talmud Ketubbot 8b)

It makes no difference whether slander is said directly to a person's face or not. (Mishneh Torah, Hilkhot De'ot 7:5)

Hot coals that are cooled on the outside grow cool within, but gossip and slander, even if cooled outwardly, do not cool inwardly.   (Jerusalem Talmud, Peah 1:1)

The person who slanders, who listens to slander, and who testifies falsely, deserves to be thrown to the dogs.
                              (Talmud Pesahim 118a)

God accepts repentance for all sins, except for the sin of imposing a bad name upon another person.(Zohar 3, 53a)

One's speech should always be clean and one's words polite.   (Talmud Pesahim 3a)

The person who is vulgar in speech descends to the deepest region of the netherworld.   (Talmud Shabbat 33a)

Try to discipline yourself not to speak too much so that you do not come to the point of uttering bad language or indecent words and do not become a chronic complainer.
              (Menorat ha-Ma'or, chapter on Lashon Hara)

If your tongue turns to uttering slander, go and study the words of Torah.   (Midrash on Psalms, Buber ed., p. 106)

If you hear something unseemly, put your hands on your ears.   (Talmud Ketubbot 5a–b)

Questions

1. How do you feel about censorship in the recording industry? Are you offended by the language used in songs today?

2. Why do so many obscene words deal with parts of the body or bodily functions? Why are these words considered obscene?

3. Here are some selected phrases from the Al Het confessional prayer recited on Yom Kippur. Read them and identify those which deal with language. Why do you believe that so many of them deal with communication?

We have missed the mark—

by being heartless	by deceit and falsehood
by the wrong way we speak	by gossiping
by wronging our neighbor	by the way we eat and drink
by confessing insincerely	by judging others too quickly
by mocking parents and	by being selfish teachers
by foul language	by being stubborn
by foolish talk	by not keeping promises

4. In a famous talmudic tale, Elijah the Prophet appears to one of the rabbis to tell him: "Never get drunk and you will not sin. Never lose your temper and you will not sin" (Talmud Berachot 29b). Do you agree with this statement? Do you think that it is possible for a person who has a strong temper to learn to control it?

5. A Hassidic teaching states that "human beings are God's language." Explain this expression.

6. Dennis Prager and Joseph Telushkin suggest that if you want to start acting Jewishly in the realm of refraining from gossip, you should—

eliminate gossip at the Shabbat dinner table on Friday night;
avoid spending time with others who constantly gossip;
change the topic with people who gossip; and
not reveal private conversations that you have with others.[4]

What do you think about these suggestions? What others might you add to help keep a person away from gossip?

7. It has been said that the words people use are often representative of their morality. What is your opinion? Discuss it with your classmates.

8. Think about the different ways suggested by the rabbis to help us train ourselves to avoid misusing language. Do you have any suggestions to add?

9. In the Elohai Netzor prayer, which concludes the everyday Amidah, there is a line that says, "To those who slander me, let me give no heed." Is it possible not to ignore someone who slanders you? How would you explain this verse?

10. During a radio broadcast a political writer once remarked, "We have to use words to talk same the way we use cooking utensils to cook." What does this statement mean? Do you agree?

11. We generally elect officials to public office on the basis of the words we hear them speak. By what criteria ought we to judge a person's words and speech?

[4]Prager, Dennis and Telushkin, Joseph *Eight Questions People Ask About Judaism* (California: Tze Ulmad Press, 1975), p. 175.

13
Honesty and Truth

Have you ever thought about what it might be like to be obliged to tell the truth for twenty-four hours? Do you think you could do it? Many have tried and failed. Some have gotten themselves into trouble in the effort.

Everyone knows the story of Pinocchio, whose nose grew every time he lied until it become grotesque. A social scientist estimates that the average American outstrips Pinocchio by telling as many as two hundred lies a day (including white lies and false excuses). Lying has become a serious problem of major proportions.

Jewish Sources On Telling The Truth

Without truth, human society and human relationships cannot long endure. A customer making a purchase has to be able to trust the seller. A homeowner has to assume that the artisan called in for a home-repair will do an honest job. A client has to believe his lawyer. A patient has to trust his doctor. Unless people tell each other the truth, our most basic relationships will disintegrate.

It is not surprising that Jewish tradition places great emphasis on the importance of telling the truth. The Torah says, "Keep far from falsehood" (Exodus 23:7). The Talmud puts it even more strongly when it says, "The Holy One hates a person who says one thing with his mouth and another in his heart" (Talmud Pesachim 113b). And after we die, said the rabbis, when each of us stands in judgment before God, the first question we will be asked is whether or not we were honest in our business dealings (Midrash on Psalm 118)

Here are some other sayings related to honesty and telling the truth.

> There is no salvation in falsehood.   (Ruth Rabbah 5:13)

> All lies are forbidden unless they are spoken for the sake of making peace.   (Bereitha)

> Teach your tongue to say "I do not know," lest you invent something and be trapped.   (Talmud Berakhot 4a)

> Nowadays falsehood stands erect and truth lies prostrate on the ground.   (Zohar 2, 88)

Two Tales About The Truth

Is there ever a time when telling the truth may not be the best policy? Is it permissible to tell white lies? Read the following case and answer the questions that accompany it.

> Case: A woman is told by a doctor that her husband is dying of a terminal disease. The patient has a maximum of one year to live under optimal conditions; there are no medical means available either to extend the life span or cure the disease.

Questions

1. Should the patient be told of the true nature of the illness, or should the truth be modified to spare him the anguish?

2. What values come into play in this decision?

3. Can you identify all of the persons whose feelings you believe ought to be taken into consideration in order to decide this case?

In the next story, we may imagine that the midrash is answering the question: "Is telling the truth always the best policy?" In other words, given a concrete situation where truth conflicts with other values, under what circumstances should it be set aside in favor of another value? The midrash attempts to answer this question by depicting a scene in which God and God's angels engage in conversation with each other.

> Rabbi Simon said: When God was about to create Adam, the ministering angels split into contending groups. Some said, "Let him be created," while others cried, "Let him not be created." That is why it is written, "Mercy and truth collided, righteousness and peace engaged in a clash" [Psalm 85:11].
>
> Mercy said, "Let him be created, for he will do merciful deeds." Truth said, "Let him not be created, for he will only lie."
>
> What did the Holy One, blessed be He, do? He took truth and cast it to the ground . . .   (Genesis Rabbah 8:5)

Questions

1. Why did truth have to be cast to the ground before man could be created?

2. Why did God choose the advice of mercy over that of truth? What would happen now if humankind was judged primarily by the standard of truth?

3. Who do you think wrote this midrash, a follower of Bet Hillel or a follower of Bet Shammai?

White Lies: Are They Ever Permissible?

The rabbis occasionally permitted white lies, especially those intended to promote peace and harmony. For example, the Talmud states, "Great is the cause of peace, seeing that for its sake even the Holy One modified a statement, for at first it is written 'with my husband so old' [Genesis 18:12], while afterwards it is written 'old as I am' [Genesis 18:13]" (Yevamot 65b). This refers to an incident in which Sarah says that both she and Abraham are too old to have children, and God, talking to Abraham, rephrases her statement to make it refer only to her own advanced age. The rabbis said that God did this so as not to give cause for quarrel between husband and wife.

Can you think of an occasion in your life when you altered the truth for the sake of peace? Do you think that a patient who has been diagnosed as terminally ill ought to be told the truth, or should the truth be modified in order to spare the patient anguish?

Three Talmudic Instances Of Telling Lies

The Talmud observes that a scholar will never tell a lie except in the three instances of "tractate," "bed," and "hospitality" (Bava Metzia 23b–24a). The commentators explain "tractate" to mean that a modest scholar is permitted to declare that he is unfamiliar with a tractate of the Mishnah in order not to flaunt his learning. "Bed" is understood to mean that if a person is asked intimate questions regarding his marital life he need not answer truthfully. "Hospitality" is understood to mean that a person who has been generously treated by a host may decide not to tell the truth about his reception if he fears that as a result the host will be embarrassed by unwelcome guests.

Questions

1. What effect does lying have on a person?

2. When do you find yourself most prone to tell a lie?

3. What would you do in this situation: You see your brother take ten dollars from your mother's purse. At dinner, your mother angrily announces that in the morning she is going to fire the cleaning woman for stealing. Your brother is silent on the matter. What would you do?

14
Stealing and Cheating

Stealing and theft constitute a most serious crime in Jewish law, as can be attested to by the fact that the prohibition in Exodus 20:13, "Do not steal," is one of the Ten Commandments. Stealing is far more prevalent than many people would care to admit. In any given year, vast amounts of merchandise are illegally removed from stores around the country. In a recent study of customer's habits in stores, five hundred shops were randomly observed. It was found that one in twelve customers stole something!

As billions of dollars worth of merchandise continues to be stolen, the cost of security escalates. It is the consumer that suffers, having to ultimately pay for lost goods by increased premiums tacked onto the price.

Obligation To Return Lost Property

Several passages in the Torah prohibit stealing and list the penalties for doing so. In addition, the Torah deals with the ethical responsibility of the finder of lost property. In all cases one can see the Torah's great concern for the preservation of the sanctity of property and the ethical duty to return lost articles.

Perhaps the best test of any person's character lies in those so-called border areas of human behavior in which either of two opposed lines of action is defensible. The reaction of someone who finds lost property belonging to another person is a good case in point. A finder can easily come up with an excuse for retaining the found property without any sense of guilt, even though such a course of action may be tantamount to robbing a fellow human being. It is for this reason that Judaism considers the return of a lost object to its rightful owner to be a positive mitzvah. Jewish law requires that the finder protect the found object and wait for its rightful owner to identify it. Here are several statements from the Torah related to the prohibition against stealing and the requirement to return lost property:

Do not steal. (Exodus 20:13)

If a person steals an ox, or a sheep, and kills it, or sells it, that person shall pay five oxen for an ox, and four sheep for a sheep. (Exodus 21:37)

If you see your neighbor's ox or sheep gone astray, do not ignore it. Take it back to your neighbor. If your neighbor does not live near you, or you do not know the owner's identity, bring it home, and it shall remain with you until your neighbor claims it. Then give it back. Do the same with an ass and with a garment. So too do the same with anything that your neighbor loses and you find. You must not remain indifferent. (Deuteronomy 22:1–3)

Questions

1. Why is there a specific law related to returning an enemy's lost property? Would you be likely to follow such a law if an opportunity presented itself?

2. How do you understand the reasoning behind the law stating that a person who steals an ox or a sheep shall pay five oxen for stealing one ox, and four sheep for stealing one sheep. What is the psychology behind this law?

Rabbinic Texts On Stealing

The rabbis had much to say about stealing. Many of the rabbinic laws of damages are cited in the tractate of the Talmud called Nezikin. Here some passages from rabbinic sources related to theft and the return of lost property. Read them and try to answer the questions that follow.

> One who robs the public must restore to the public. Worse is stealing from the public than stealing from a single individual, for one who steals from an individual can appease that individual and return the theft. The former cannot do this.   (Tosefta Bava Kamma 10:14)

> You must not steal, even if it be done merely to annoy or even to restore double or fourfold or fivefold. Ben Bag Bag said: "You must not steal your own property back from a thief, lest you appear to be stealing."   (Sifra 38b)

> What is considered lost property? [Something found where it was not supposed to be.] If one found a donkey or a cow grazing on the way, it is not lost property. If one, however, finds a donkey and its burden topsy-turvy, or a cow running through a vineyard, this is obviously lost property.   (Mishnah Bava Metzia 2:9)

The following articles [automatically] belong to the finder: if one finds scattered fruit, scattered money, small sheaves in a public thoroughfare, round cakes of pressed figs, a baker's loaves, strings of fish, pieces of meat, fleeces of wool which have been brought from the country, bundles of flax, and stripes of purple-colored wool—all these belong to the finder.   (Mishneh Bava Metzia 2:1)

In order to retrieve a lost object, the owner must be able to clearly identify it. If the object does not possess any distinctive markings, then it automatically belongs to the finder.   (Mishneh Bava Metzia 2:7)

Questions

1. Based on the preceding laws, what do you think constitutes a lost object according to the rabbis?

2. According to the rabbis, under what circumstances may a person who discovers a lost object invoke the principle of "finders—keepers"? What is your principle for finders—keepers?

3. Do you agree with the rabbinic principle that if a lost object has no distinctive markings it should automatically belong to the finder? Can you think of an exception to this rule?

4. Here is a list of objects. Which, according to the rabbis, would be considered lost property?

a. Money washed up on the shores of a beach.
b. A sweater found in your school gym.
c. A twenty-dollar bill found on the floor next to a bank's ATM.
d. A bracelet at the bottom of a swimming pool.
e. A watch on the rooftop of your house.

5. Here is a hypothetical case that deals with a loss. How would you decide it, based up your reading and understanding of rabbinic sources?

> Kathy was babysitting for the Jones family. Her rate was four dollars per hour, and she sat for the Jones family for a period of five hours. When the Joneses returned, Mrs. Jones drove Kathy home. When they reached Kathy's house, Mrs. Jones handed her an envelope with money. Without ever looking at it, Kathy entered her home. Imagine Kathy's surprise when upon opening the envelope, she found that she had been given a fifty-dollar bill.

Deception: Stealing Of The Mind

There is another kind of theft—the kind that occurs when you deceive another person. In Hebrew this kind of stealing is called *geneivat da'at,* literally, "stealing the mind" of the other person. Among other things, it applies to the bait and switch tricks that some retailers utilize. They advertise a certain product at an amazingly discounted price; when customers come to the store expecting to purchase the item at the advertised price, they claim that the product is unavailable, substituting a high-priced product in its place. *Geneivat da'at* also occurs when a used-car dealer dresses up a vehicle or turns back its odometer to make it appear newer than it really is.

Here are some examples of deception from rabbinic sources. Read them and then do the exercise that follows:

> There are seven kinds of thieves, and the first of them is the one who steals the mind of another human being. Examples of deceivers are the person who urges a neighbor to be his guest but in his heart does not mean to invite him. Or the person who shoves gifts upon a neighbor when he knows that the neighbor will not accept them.
> (Tosefta Bava Kamma 8)

As there is wrongdoing or cheating in buying and selling, so there is also wrongdoing in words. One must not ask the price of an object if one has no real intention of buying it. (Talmud, Bab Metzia 58b)

Rabbi Meir said, "Do not press your neighbor to eat with you when you know that your neighbor will not accept the invitation." (Tosefta Bava Batra 6:14)

Rabbi Meir said: "Do not buy vessels with money borrowed for the purpose of buying fruit, or vice versa, because in so doing you steal the mind of the lender."
(Tosefta Megillah 1:5)

One is forbidden to dye a slave's beard or hair in order to make him appear young. . . . One is not allowed to paint old baskets to make them appear new, nor to soak meat in water to make it look white and fat.
(Code of Jewish Law, Hoshen Mishpat 358)

Exercises

How would you decide the following cases based upon the rabbinic texts on deception?

Lori dated Barry several times, and he took her to fancy nightclubs. However, she decided that his personality was not quite right for her and decided never to accept another date with him again. Several weeks later Barry called to tell Lori her that he had two tickets for a well-known Broadway play which she had always wanted to see.

Do you think that Lori should accept Barry's invitation? If yes, is she guilty of the crime of stealing his mind?

Bill had some time to kill at the mall. He went into a electronics store and asked the salesperson to show him a wide array of devices, with no real intention of ever buying anything.

Do you think that Bill is guilty of mental theft?

> You are the school board chairperson for your synagogue and have recently decided to terminate the contract of your youth director. The youth director, in seeking another position, uses your name as a reference. You are called by an officer of the congregation offering the position and asked about him.

What would you say? How truthful do you think you would be?

Cheating: Another Form of Theft

There is much concern nowadays about the morals of young people. A study by the Girl Scouts of America on the beliefs and values of girls and boys ages nine through eighteen included the following finding: sixty-five percent of the high school students said that they would probably cheat in some way on a test rather than do poorly, especially if they did not have enough time to study.

Cheating is a kind of stealing, in this case the stealing of another person's ideas. Cheating is on the rise in our society. Some parents encourage their children to cheat if it means getting ahead. A recent West Coast study asked thirty thousand college freshmen whether they had ever cheated on a test in their senior year in high school. The results showed that thirty-three percent said that they had cheated.

Is cheating human nature, or do parents, teachers, and other members of society encourage it by their own attitudes? Some psychologists say that cheating is inevitable among young children, because their morality is centered on the idea that whatever brings good or better results is right.

Questions

1. If you were taking a test and saw the student next to you glancing over at your paper, what would you do?

2. Can you think of a situation in which cheating might be morally permissible?

3. What might you say to your own child in order to instill the value of being honest and not cheating?

15
Social Justice

The Torah commands, "Justice, justice shall you pursue" (Deuteronomy 16:20). This is usually interpreted to mean that we must *actively* pursue justice, and that our means of pursuing it must themselves be just. In Judaism, justice is defined as dealing fairly with others. It does not simply concern our personal encounters, but also compels our active involvement with broader issues of social justice, including justice for the mentally ill, the disabled, and the disadvantaged.

For Jews, righteousness is not merely an attitude of benevolence toward our fellow human beings, but an *obligatory* act, a mitzvah! Indeed, the record of Jewish social action activities in our country continues an illustrious chapter in the long and varied history of the Jewish people in the field of social service. Jews to this day persist in believing in our divinely appointed role to bring all people to a recognition of God's moral standard.

This chapter will enable you to explore the ethics of social justice by comparing the actions of two biblical personalities who are known for their goodness and righteousness, Noah and Abraham. In the lives of both a catastrophe arose, and each of them was required to deal with it in his own way. You will be asked to judge both men and decide for yourself which one assumed the highest degree of moral responsibility.

The Story of Noah

This is the line of Noah. Noah was a righteous man, blameless in his age. Noah walked with God. The earth became corrupt before God and was filled with lawlessness. When God saw how corrupt the earth was, for all flesh had corrupted its ways on earth, God said to Noah, "I have decided to put an end to all flesh. Make yourself an ark of gopher wood." Then God added, "But I will establish My covenant with you, and you shall enter the ark, with your sons, your wife, and your sons' wives. And of all that lives, of all flesh, you shall take two of each into the ark to keep alive with you—they shall be male and female."

Noah took his wife, his sons, and their wives into the ark, along with all of the animals. When the waters had swelled much more upon the earth, all the highest mountains everywhere under the sky were covered. And all flesh that stirred on earth perished—all the animals and all of humankind. Only Noah was left, and those with him in the ark.

God blessed Noah and his sons, and said to them, "Be fertile and increase, and fill the earth." And God further said, "I now establish My covenant with you and your offspring to come. And this is the covenant. I have set My rainbow in the clouds, and it shall serve as a sign of the covenant between Me and the earth. When I bring clouds over the earth, and the rainbow appears in the clouds, I will remember My covenant between Me and you and every living creature, so that the water shall never again become a flood to destroy all flesh."

(summarized from Genesis 6:9–9:28)

Questions

In the course of answering the questions in this section, you may wish to keep in mind these five sources which have a bearing upon our moral obligations to others:

> All Israel are guarantors one for another.
> (Talmud Sanhedrin 27b)

> Hillel said: "Do not separate yourself from the community."
> (Pirke Avot 2:5)

> Do not stand idly by the blood of your neighbor.
> (Leviticus 19:16)

> Therefore was only one person created, to teach you that whosoever wrecks a single soul, the Bible considers to have wrecked a complete world, and whosoever sustains and saves a single soul, it is as if that person sustained a whole world.
> (Mishneh Sanhedrin 4:5)

> If I am not for myself, who will be for me. If I am only for myself, what am I? If not now, when?   (Pirke Avot 1:14)

1. The Torah says that "Noah was a righteous person in his generation" (Genesis 6:9). According to some commentators, this means that Noah can be regarded as righteous only when compared to the other members of his generation but would not have been considered righteous in other eras. Other commentators say it means that Noah was righteous in his own generation and would have been even more so in other ages. In your opinion, what did the Torah mean when it called Noah a person "righteous in his generation"? What does the word "righteous" mean to you?

2. Do you know anyone whom you would classify as righteous? If so, what are their moral virtues? Do you consider any historical figure to have been a righteous person?

3. In modern times it is difficult to conceive of a situation in which a person might take an ethical stand in opposition to that of the society in which he lives. Here is one parallel:

Five high school students out of a hundred taking a science exam refuse to cheat or share information, even though there is no teacher in the room and most everyone else is cheating.

What is especially difficult about the moral situation of Noah and of the students in the situation just described? Can you think of a time in your own life in which someone was about to take such a position? Describe it.

4. What does the Noah story tell us about God's morality?

5. If you had been in Noah's position, do you think that you would have done the same things he did, or would you have reacted some other way when God asked you to build an ark?

6. Is there such a thing as a universally accepted law of morality, whereby all people believe that something is right and just? Why or why not?

7. Did Noah's character have any shortcomings? On a scale of 1 to 10, with 1 being the lowest, how would you rate Noah's ethics?

The Story of Abraham and Sodom

God appeared to Abraham by the terebinths of Mamre. Abraham was sitting at the entrance of the tent as the day grew hot. Looking up, he saw three men standing near him. As soon as he saw them, he ran from the entrance of the tent to greet them, and bowing to the ground, he said, "My lords, if it please you, do not go past your servant. Let some water be brought, bathe your feet, and recline under the tree. And let me fetch you some broth so that you can refresh yourselves."

Abraham hastened into the tent to Sarah and said,

"Quick, make cakes!" Then Abraham ran to the herd, took a calf, and set it before them.

The men set out from there and looked down toward Sodom, Abraham walking with them to see them off. Now God said, "Shall I hide from Abraham what I am about to do, since Abraham is to become a great and populous nation, and all the nations of the earth are to bless themselves by them? For I have singled him out, that he may instruct his children and his posterity to keep the way of God by doing what is just and right, in order that God may bring about for Abraham what He has promised him."

Then God said, "The outrage of Sodom and Gomorrah is so great, and their sin is so grave! I will go down to see whether they have acted altogether according to the outcry that has come to Me."

The men went on from there to Sodom, while Abraham remained standing before God. Abraham came forward and said, "God, will You sweep away the innocent along with the guilty? What if there should be fifty innocent within the city. Will You still wipe out the place and not forgive it for the sake of the innocent fifty who are in it? Far be it from You to do such a thing, to bring death upon the innocent as well as the guilty, so that innocent and guilty fare alike. Far be it from You. Shall not the Judge of all the earth deal justly?"

And God answered, "If I find within the city of Sodom fifty innocent ones, I will forgive the whole place for their sake."

And Abraham spoke up, saying, "What if the fifty innocent shall lack five? Will You destroy the city for want of five? God replied, "I will not destroy if I find forty-five there."

But he spoke to God again and said, "What if forty should be found there?" God answered, "I will not do it, for the sake of forty."

And Abraham said, "Let not my God be angry if I go on. What if thirty should be found there?" God answered, "I will not do it if I find thirty there."

Abraham said, "What if twenty should be found there?" God answered, "I will not destroy for the sake of the twenty."

And Abraham said, "Let not my God be angry if I speak but this last time. What if ten should be found there?" God answered, "I will not destroy for the sake of the ten."

When God had finished speaking to Abraham, He departed. Abraham returned to his place.

(based on Genesis 18)

Questions

1. Do you think that Abraham doubted God's justice? Have you ever had doubts or questions about something God did?

2. Abraham is pleading not merely for the innocent but for the sinners, because if the city is spared for the sake of the righteous people who live there, the sinners will also be saved. If you were God, would you have spared all of the people of Sodom and Gomorrah because of the merit of a few righteous individuals?

3. Could God have destroyed Sodom and Gomorrah and still have been just to all the people concerned?

4. Why didn't Abraham warn the people of Sodom and Gomorrah of their impending doom?

5. How do you think Noah would have acted if he had faced the situation of Sodom and Gomorrah?

6. The midrash on Deuteronomy 11:3 compares Abraham, Moses, and Noah to decide which of them was the greater. In one portion of the text, the following is cited:

Abraham said to Moses, "I am greater than you, because I used to give hospitality to all passers-by." Whereupon Moses replied, "I am far superior to you. You fed uncircumcised men, but I fed circumcised ones. And further,

you gave hospitality in an inhabited land, but I fed them
in the wilderness."

What criteria do you use when you are evaluating a person's
greatness? How much value do you place on the person's
social ethics?

7. How would you rate Abraham's righteousness and social
ethics as compared to Noah's? Who took the greater risk?
Who was the better person?

8. The prophet Isaiah said that the Israelites were to become
a "light to all of the nations" (Isaiah 42:6). What does this
phrase mean? In what way can you be a light to other people?

9. What social services/social action organizations do you
have in your community? Which ones do you have in your
own congregation? What successes have they achieved?

16
In God's Image: Human Sexuality

Jewish Perspectives on the Body

In the opening chapters of the Book of Genesis we learn that God created the first man and woman in God's own image. Many have interpreted this to mean that we should use our bodies for divine purposes. Since its pleasures are God-given, the body can and should be a source of holiness. In this, Judaism differs markedly from Christianity, which holds that the soul of a living being is the divine part, while the body, the animal part, imprisons the soul and prevents it from joining God.

Another implication of the creation of humankind is that our bodies were given to us by God and in a sense are on loan to us for the duration of our lives. Thus we are expected to take proper care of our bodies and keep ourselves in the best of health. Here are several Jewish sources about the body:

> Since it is the will of the Almighty that our bodies be kept healthy and strong, because it is impossible for us to have any knowledge of our Creator when ill, it is therefore

115

our duty to shun anything which may waste our body, and to strive to acquire habits that will help us to become healthy. Thus it is written "Take good care of your souls" [Deuteronomy 4:15].

(Code of Jewish Law, chap. 32)

Our rabbis, of blessed memory, said: "Which is a short verse upon which all the principles of Torah depend? It is 'In all ways we must acknowledge Him' [Proverbs 3:6]" [Berakhot 63a]. This means that in all of our actions, even those we do in order to sustain life, we must acknowledge God, and do them for the sake of His name. For instance, eating, drinking, walking, sitting, lying down, rising, having sexual intercourse, talking—all acts performed to sustain life should be done for the sake of worshipping our Creator, or doing something that will be conducive to the service of God.   (Code of Jewish Law, chap. 31)

Praised are You, God, who has with wisdom created human beings and has fashioned within them large and small openings. It is revealed and known before Your holy throne that if just one of these were perforated or obstructed, it would be impossible to survive before You. Praised are You, God, who heals all creatures and does wonders.

(Prayer traditionally recited after going to bathroom)

Questions

1. What is the basic premise of the preceding texts? How do they compare with the view of today's popular culture?

2. How do you feel about this view?

3. What are some ways to make our bodies holy?

4. Do you believe that our bodies are on loan to us from God?

5. Judaism has always valued modesty. How might the value of modesty apply to one's body?

Judaism and Sex

Judaism is a religion to live by. It offers guidance in all areas of life. Thus it ought not to come as a surprise that there is a Jewish way to think about sex and a Jewish way to have sex. Sex is one of the gifts that God has given us by creating us as we are. Like all of our faculties, we can use it for good or for bad. I'd like to share with you an amazing story which I first read when I was a teenager studying in my local Hebrew high school. It appears in the Talmud:

> Rabbi Kahana once went and hid under [his teacher] Rav's bed. He heard him speaking with his wife and joking and doing what he required. He [Kahana] said to him, "One surely would think that Abba never sipped the dish before." He [Abba] said to him, "Kahana, are you here? Get out, because it is rude." Kahana replied, "It is a matter of Torah, and I need to learn." (Berakhot 62a)

Obviously my teacher did not recommend that I go out and hide under my rabbi's bed to see how he was making love. However, this story clearly provides us with insight, for it shows how far a student was willing to go to learn the proper Jewish lovemaking techniques.

Although the Bible and rabbinic law do not lay out an organized sex ethic for us, they do hint at attitudes toward sex. Here are several sources from the Bible and the Talmud that begin to paint a Jewish attitude toward sex and its ethics:

> God blessed Adam and Eve and said, "Be fertile and multiply and fill the earth."   (Genesis 1:28)

Here we clearly see that sex was to be a part of God's master plan, and that it was also one of the purposes of marriage.

> Thus a man leaves his father and mother and clings to his wife, so that they become one flesh. (Genesis 2:21–24)

From this verse we see that it is not good for people to be alone, and that companionship through marriage is an important goal in life.

> None of you shall come near anyone of his own flesh to uncover nakedness, I am the Lord.   (Leviticus 18:6)

This passage, which is followed by a long list of forbidden sexual relationships, is read at the afternoon Minhah service on Yom Kippur, the holiest day of the year. It is intended to impress upon young people the need to maintain Israel's high standard of chastity and family morality. Impurity in marriage, incestuous promiscuity among near-relations, and other abominations are condemned and regarded as unpardonable sins.

> If a man is found lying with another man's wife, both of them, the man and the woman with whom he lay, shall die. Thus you will sweep away evil from Israel.
>
> (Deuteronomy 22:22–24)

Here we see the biblical penalty for a married man who has relations with another woman.

Questions

1. In what ways can the sex act hurt and destroy a person?
2. Define sexual immorality.

Is Living Together Immoral?

Popular culture has reinforced a casual acceptance of sex outside of marriage. Modern developments in birth control and prophylaxis have removed two fears that once served to inhibit sex among people who were not married to each other: pregnancy and disease.

The Torah itself never explicitly forbids nonmarital sex (except in the cases of adultery and incest). It was the rabbis who later forbade it, primarily because of its potential to undermine marriage. If holiness was to be the Jewish ideal, then every effort had to be made to sanctify sex by limiting it to a marital relationship of loving partners.

For teenagers, it is often the case that the body is ready to have sex but the emotions are not. The classical answer in Judaism was to arrange for an early marriage. Today, early marriage is not practicable.

There are two major patterns of extramarital sexual relationships—premarital and nonmarital. Premarital relationships involve couples who have made a definite commitment to marry in the foreseeable future. They may even be formally engaged. Nonmarital sexual relations involve a agreement between two parties, on either a short-term or a long-term basis, to engage in sexual relations with no commitment to marry. As both of these types of relationships are more and more accepted in today's society, many Jews are challenging the traditional view of such practices. Judaism itself has noticed these patterns of sexual behavior at different times in our history. Beginning in early biblical times, Judaism was in conflict with its Canaanite neighbors, who used sex as part of their religious cult. Judaism forbade cultic sexual intercourse.

The term for a Jewish wedding is *kiddushin,* which means "sanctification." This expression reflects the spirituality and holiness that are an integral part of a husband-wife relationship. Judaism sees marriage as an expression of total commitment between two persons. And it has traditionally seen sexual intercourse as the ultimate expression of communication and love rather than the basis on which love is supposed to grow.

Questions

1. How do you know when a relationship is based on love and not just sexual attraction?

2. Here is a biblical excerpt dealing with a relationship. After reading it, state what kind of love and sexual attraction it portrays.

> And Isaac went out walking in the field toward evening and, looking up, he saw camels approaching. Raising her eyes, Rebekkah saw Isaac. She alighted from the camel and said to the servant, "Who is the man walking in the field toward us?" And the servant said, "It is my master." So she took her veil and covered herself. The servant told Isaac all the things that he had done. Isaac then brought her into the tent of his mother Sarah, and he took Rebekkah as his wife. Isaac loved her, and thus found comfort after his mother's death.   (Genesis 24:63–67)

3. Role-play the following situation: A rabbi is counseling an unmarried couple who have been living together for one year. They are having problems in their relationship. Have one person take the part of the rabbi and two others play the couple. After a few minutes, stop and debrief by answering this question: How do the unmarried couple's concerns differ from those of a married couple?

4. Suppose you were a rabbi and someone asked you for a set of Jewish guidelines about how to behave sexually prior to marriage. What would you suggest?

1._____

2._____

3._____

4._____

5._____

5. Rabbi Elliot Dorff has written that "teenagers need to refrain from sexual intercourse, for they cannot honestly deal with its implications or results—including the commitments and responsibilities that sexual relations imply, the possibility of children, and the risk of AIDS and other sexually transmitted diseases. Abstinence is surely not easy when the physical and social pressures are strong, but it is the only responsible thing to do."[5]

What is your reaction to this statement? Do you agree with any part of it?

6. A psychiatrist once described a young girl, one of his patients, as saying, "I believe one should have intercourse only when in love, so I am constantly in love." Do you know anyone who acts on this premise?

[5]Dorff, Elliot "Jewish Pastoral Letter," (Los Angeles: University of Judaism, 1994), p. 29.

7. Bill and Jean are one month away from their marriage ceremony. They have spent one particular Sunday on a skiing trip, and after a fun day and a wonderful dinner, they are ready to retire for the night. Jean is surprised to find herself suggesting to Bill that they should spend the night together. "We've waited a long time," she says to him. "We love each other."

Will one month really make a difference in terms of their abstaining from sexual intercourse? Will the future happiness of Bill and Jean be affected by the decision they make now? How?

8. Do you believe in "love at first sight"?

9. Some people say that living together is a good testing ground for marriage. Do you agree or disagree? Why?

10. When you become seriously interested in another person, how can you distinguish between infatuation and love? Between sexual attraction and an emotion that leads to an enduring partnership?

11. Here is a definition of love by Alexander Magoun, a leading marriage counselor and sociologist. After reading it, answer these questions:

> Love is a feeling of tenderness and devotion toward someone, so profound that to share that individual's joy, anticipations, sorrow and pain is the very essence of living. Love is the passionate and abiding desire on the part of two people . . . to produce together the conditions under which each can be himself or herself, and spontaneously express his real self; to produce together an intellectual soil and an emotional climate in which each can flourish, far superior to what either could achieve alone.

a. Do you agree with the definition? b. Can you improve upon the definition? c. What factors does Magoun emphasize?

17
Intermarriage: Should I or Shouldn't I?

Why Is Marriage Within The Faith So Important?

A cry of anguish reached us from a rabbi in a southwestern city. "Woe," he wrote, "we are intermarrying out of existence." The 1990 National Jewish Population Survey, conducted by the Council of Jewish Federations, shocked many of us into an awareness of the great increase in intermarriage over the last decade. The statistics are staggering. Of every four Jews who marry, two are marrying non-Jews. Because of these developments, many Jews have become deeply concerned about intermarriage. The topic has spilled out beyond the Jewish community and has become a matter for public discussion.

Judaism has always stressed the importance of marrying within the faith and preserving its heritage of culture and traditions. Differences of religion often constitute a serious obstacle to harmonious husband-wife relationships. Even when mixed marriages endure, they often impose a strain on the religious loyalties of one or both partners, and can cause difficult personal and family problems.

The earliest biblical story about the importance of marrying within the faith relates to Abraham, Judaism's first patriarch.

Abraham sends his servant Eliezer to find a suitable wife for his son Isaac, admonishing him with these words: "I will make you swear that you will not take a wife for my son from the daughters of the Canaanites among whom I dwell, but you will go to the land of my birth and get a wife for my son" (Genesis 24:3–4).

This is the first biblical mention of opposition to mixed marriage. In a second biblical story, Isaac charges his son Jacob not to take a wife from among the Canaanites, a non-Israelite people inhabiting ancient Palestine (Genesis 28:1).

Question

Why do you think that both Abraham and Isaac did not want their sons to marry women who were not from their people?

If Abraham and Isaac did not clearly explain why they were opposed to mixed marriages, no room is left for guesswork when the Book of Deuteronomy restates the matter in legal terms. It warns the Israelites that when they come to the Promised Land and become acquainted with its inhabitants, they are not to intermarry with them, for that will turn their children away from God (Deuteronomy 7:1–4). The Bible is warning here that mixed marriages pose a threat to Jewish survival.

The strongest biblical denunciation of mixed marriage is found in the Book of Ezra, written soon after the return from the Babylonian Exile. The practice of mixed marriage had become quite common. Ezra did not simply denounce it. He ordered all intermarried Jews to divorce their gentile wives (Ezra 9:12–14).

Questions

1. What problems do mixed marriages pose for Judaism?

2. What are some of the reasons for the increased rate of intermarriage today?

3. Many young Jews who marry gentiles consider intermarriage and retaining their Jewishness to be mutually consistent. If this is the case, then what do you think being Jewish means to them?

Interdating

Does mixed dating lead to Jewish-gentile marriage? One thing is certain: the intermarriage rate among those who never dated a non-Jew is zero. Most of you who are reading this book are not likely to be contemplating marriage in your immediate future. But the older you get, the more realistic the question of the type of person to marry will become.

Will dating out of the faith on a regular basis increase your chances of establishing a permanent relationship with a person who is not Jewish? One would certainly think so, since dating is the process of sorting out our feelings about members of the opposite sex, establishing patterns of socialization, and delineating our group of friends. Is there anything morally wrong in a Jew's dating a non-Jew? Not really, but there is something explosively dangerous about it, since no one decides in advance when and with whom to fall in love. Thus, the more one grows accustomed to dating partners out of the faith, the greater the possibility that when love finally does arrive, the other member of the cast will be of a faith different from your own.

My students have often argued that romantic relationships in high school do not persist through the years to the point of marriage. In my twenty-five years as a rabbi in one community, I have seen many high school romances result in marriage. The path of wisdom, then, if you do not wish to completely rule out dating non-Jews, is to keep these contacts on as casual a basis as possible. Certainly the more frequently you date fellow Jews, the more likely it is that later down the line you will marry within the Jewish faith.

Young people who are dating often begin to look for commitments and values that they would want to see in a future spouse. When you think you have found someone who would make the kind of marriage partner you are seeking, you need to determine whether the two of you share the same commitments and values. The more values and concerns you have in common, the greater the likelihood of a happy marriage. If you marry within the faith, you are certainly more likely to find common values because of our common heritage.

In Summation

Aside from the important consideration of marital harmony, Judaism opposes mixed marriage because it poses a threat to the future of the Jewish people, and to their faith, customs, and traditions. The Jewish people are and always have been a minority. Seeking to preserve their group identity, they find it crucial to resist the inroads of mixed marriage. Dating patterns often determine the kind of marriage partner one finally selects. The more Jewish dates you have, the more likely that you will marry within the Jewish faith. The choice is yours.

What are the Advantages of a Jewish Marriage?

Marriages today are difficult enough without the added problem of differing values and religions. There are many advantages to a Jewish marriage over a mixed marriage. Two Jewish partners will be able to share the warmth and strength of Jewish customs and observances, song and prayer, food, literature, and the like, without the need for constant explanation and interpretation. The children of a Jewish couple will not be torn between two religious traditions, nor will they be denied religious training because of conflicting beliefs, a situation that can sometimes lead to total avoidance. Growing up in any household with two faiths, and having to choose one over the other, can be very difficult. When young people raised in mixed-marriage households set out to establish their own religious identities, they often feel as if they are being forced to choose one parent over another.

In a Jewish marriage, the aspirations of the Jewish people as a whole become part of the shared goals of the two partners. Together, they are able to fashion a moral life and participate in the religious and cultural life of the Jewish people. Finally, by establishing a Jewish marriage, they will be helping to assure the continuity of Judaism and the Jewish people.

Questions

1. What, if anything, have your parents told you about dating someone out of the faith? What would you tell your own children?

2. How important is religion in selecting a marriage partner? Rank the criteria (in order of importance) of what you are looking for in a spouse.

3. Role-play the following situation: Mr. and Mrs. Cohen are Jewish, but have never made Judaism an important part

of their lives. One day they learn that their daughter Ruth has begun to date a non-Jew named Bill. Ruth wants to invite Bill home, but her parents object, saying that they are very unhappy with her selection of a non-Jewish date. Have two persons play Mr. and Mrs. Cohen and another play Ruth.

Why are Mr. and Mrs. Cohen so upset with Ruth's choice of Bill, especially in light of the fact that Judaism has not been an important part of their lives? What does this tell us about their feelings related to Jewishness?

4. John says he will date and marry the person with whom he falls in love. Although his parents have stressed the importance of his dating and marrying someone Jewish, John says that Judaism has no meaning for him. A few days later, John learns of a major disaster in a hospital in Israel which has been invaded by a terrorist. Israel is seeking volunteers to assist. John reacts emotionally to this plea, and before long is on a plane to Israel.

What does this scenario tell us about John and his Jewishness? Why is John so taken by this particular cause?

5. On the basis of what things do you judge the importance of Judaism in your own life?

6. How important do you think your remaining Jewish and having a Jewish family is to the survival of the Jewish people as a whole?

7. Which would you choose?

a.   Central to my being Jewish is:
         Following God's commandments.
         Avoid marrying out of the faith.
         Working to help the State of Israel.
         Helping to improve society.

b.   I think that the most serious problem facing the Jewish community today is:

Anti-semitism.
Survival of Israel.
Assimilation.
Intermarriage.
Finding Judaism directly relevant to its life.

8. Sentence completions:

a. Jewish parents, as compared to non-Jewish parents, are:

_____

_____

b. If my child wanted to seriously date a non-Jew, I would:

_____

_____

c. If my child wanted to marry a non-Jew, I would _____

_____

_____

d. If my children were to decide they no longer wanted to be Jews, I: _____

_____

_____

e. Comparing myself to my parents, my Jewish life is: _____

_____

_____

9. You have made friends with a very nice non-Jewish person in your tennis class. You are attracted to him/her, and want to go out on a date in order to become better acquainted. At the restaurant on your first date, you learn that your date is very disturbed because you are a Jew and was taught as a

child that the Jews killed Jesus. How would you react? Would you still continue to date such a person?

10. It is sometimes alleged that Jews are racists because they insist—and have insisted since the beginning of their history—that Jews should only marry Jews. How would you respond to someone who holds this opinion?

11. Some Jewish parents tell their children, "Interdate as much as possible, but don't dare marry a non-Jew." How do you feel about this attitude? Are such parents being hypocritical?

12. An old adage has it that "opposites attract." Do you agree? If so, is this a reason for a Jew to marry a non-Jew?

13. What is your answer? I would marry a non-Jew:

    a. If I loved him/her.
    b. If I could remain a Jew.
    c. If s/he converted to Judaism.
    d. Under no circumstances.
    e. Other?

18
Hatred: Is There a Jewish Response?

On Saturday, November 4, 1995, Yitzhak Rabin was assassinated by a young man, a fellow Jew, who was present at a peace rally where Rabin participated and spoke. Do you remember where you were and how you felt when you learned that Rabin had been killed? What was your reaction when you learned that he had been killed not by an Arab terrorist but by a fellow Jew? How would you have reacted if Rabin had been assassinated by an Arab?

Although scores of people of good will on all sides of the political issues have condemned the assassination, there remains a tide of extremist rhetoric and violence perpetuating the hatred that some people had for Rabin's attempt to make peace. The anger of the man who eventually killed Rabin was so out of control, and his hatred for him so deep, that he was able to do the unthinkable—murder the democratically elected leader of the State of Israel.

What does Judaism have to say about controlling one's anger and taking the law into one's own hands? This chapter will deal with these issues, as well as with Judaism's attitude in general toward hatred.

Taking the Law into One's Own Hands

In Judaism, one is bound to follow the rules and procedures of the law. The only time taking the law into one's own hands is permitted, even to the point of killing another person, is if one clearly sees a murder taking place and there is absolutely no other way to stop it. However, if there is a chance of stopping the murder in a less dramatic way, that would be preferable.

A famous biblical case of a man taking the law into his own hands is Moses. In Exodus, chapter 2, Moses sees an Egyptian beating a Hebrew slave. Moses kills the Egyptian and hides the body in the sand. The text does not reveal whether Moses killed the man deliberately or whether he beat him so severely that he died.

In a midrash on this text, we learn that when Moses reached the end of his life he tried to stave off death. God said to him, "Did I tell you to slay the Egyptian?" Moses answered, "You slew all of the firstborn in Egypt." Then God silenced him by saying, "Can you liken yourself to Me? I cause death, but I also revive the dead."

From this midrash we see that the rule of not taking the law into one's own hands applied even to Moses, the greatest of the prophets.

Questions

1. When would it be right to take the law into your own hands?

2. When, if ever, is it right to break the law?

3. Many years ago several rabbis marched for civil rights with Martin Luther King, Jr. Some were beaten and jailed. Do you think that these rabbis were acting responsibly? Were they taking the law into their own hands?

4. How do you deal with someone unreasonable?

5. When someone pressures you to do something, how do

you decide whether or not to do it?

Anger: The Jewish Attitude

What makes you angry? How do you express your anger? How do you control it? Many rabbinic statement relate to anger, its control, and its potential hazards. After reading the following quotations, answer the questions.

All angry people are fools.   (Ecclesiastes Rabbah 12:14)

An angry person's speech is like the water which overflows from a boiling kettle.   (Ecclesiastes Rabbah 7:9)

Do not grow angry, and you will not sin . . .
(Talmud Berakhot 29)

Rabbi Simeon ben Levi said: "A sage who indulges in anger loses his knowledge."   (Talmud Pesahim 66a)

An angry person is unfit to pray.
(Rabbi Nachman of Bratslav)

A gentle answer turns away wrath, but harsh words stir up anger.   (Proverbs 15:1)

All the divisions of hell rule over the angry person.
(Talmud Nedarim 22a)

Hillel used to say, "An angry person cannot be a teacher."   (Pirke Avot 2:6)

Our character can be judged by the way we handle three things: drink, money, and anger.   (Talmud Eruvin 65b)

Who is a hero? The person who controls his impulses.
(Pirke Avot 4:1)

A person who tears his clothes out of anger and shatters his utensils out of anger and scatters his coins out of anger should be considered like one who worships idols. This is the nature of the evil urge: today it says, "Do this," and tomorrow it says, "Do that," until eventually it says, "Go and worship idols," and he does that too.

(Talmud Shabbat 105b)

Questions

1. What are the most acceptable ways of expressing anger?

2. Are there ever times when you should have gotten angry but did not?

3. The last quotation in the preceding section describes how anger literally changes a person's mindset. Can you think of a modern-day example?

4. How do you control your anger? Is it possible to control your emotions if you have strong feelings about something?

Hatred

By and large, Judaism denounces hatred. "What is hateful to you, do not do to others," stated the rabbis (Talmud Shabbat 31a). The most vicious form of hatred, according to the Jewish tradition, is gratuitous hatred (*sinat hinnam*), or hatred without cause. This was considered hatred of the worst kind, and the rabbis always denounced it in extreme terms.

The following selections from traditional Jewish texts all pertain to the topic of hatred. Read them and try to answer the questions that follow.

> You shall not hate your brother in your heart.
>> (Leviticus 19:17)

1. What does this verse mean to you?
2. What does the Torah mean by "your brother"?

———————

> If you hate another person, and have not spoken to that person for three days, you are ineligible to serve as a judge in cases involving your enemy.
>> (Talmud Sanhedrin 27b)

1. On what assumptions is thus law based? Do you agree?
2. What does this law tells us about hatred?

———————

> Hatred without cause is as wicked as idolatry, adultery, and murder combined. (Talmud Yoma 9)

1. Do you agree that hatred without cause is such a grave crime?

2. Have you ever hated without cause?

3. What prompts a person to hate something or someone without apparent cause?

———————

If two people claim your help, and one is your enemy,
help your enemy first.   (Talmud Bava Metzia 32b)

1. Why would the rabbis want us to help our enemy?

2. How hard would it be to follow this halakhah?

3. What does this halakhah tell us about rabbinic thought related to personal enemies?

The fear of God is to hate evil.   (Proverbs 8:13)

1. What does this verse mean?

2. How can you act on this injunction?

Hate is like the plank of a bridge. Once in place, it stays there.   (Talmud Sanhedrin 7a)

1. Do you agree with this statement?

2. How can we rid ourselves of hatred toward another person?

I have no pleasure in the death of the wicked, but that the wicked turn away from his way and live.
                                        (Ezekiel 33:11)

What does this verse suggest about how we ought to feel about haters?

> Be like the disciples of Aaron, loving peace and pursuing peace, loving your fellow creatures and drawing near to the Torah. (Pirke Avot 1:12)

1. Is it possible to pursue peaceful dialogue with a hater?

2. What should our approach be with people who hate us or other ethnic groups?

> There is a time to love, and a time to hate.
> (Ecclesiastes 3:8)

Can you think of a right time to hate?

1. Can you think of a time when you felt you hated someone, but in retrospect the hatred was senseless and without cause?

2. What causes people to hate gratuitously?

It is usually assumed that people hate those who are identified as their enemies. The Ethics of the Fathers states that a good leader is a person who can turn an enemy into as friend (Avot de Rabbi Natan, chapter 23).

Do you think it is possible to do this? How?

A cantor who received numerous phone calls from a man named Larry Trapp, a neo-Nazi and grand dragon of the White Knights of the Ku Klu Klan. Trapp was also a paraplegic. Being persistent, the cantor was able to establish a relationship with Trapp, who eventually converted to Judaism.

What does this story tell us about the role of friendship over hatred?

Unit IV
How Do I Begin to Act More Jewishly?

When Franz Rosenzweig, a twentieth-century philosopher and theologian, was asked if he put on tefillin, he answered with two words: "Not yet." At that point in Rosenzweig's life, he was not spiritually ready and prepared to take on this mitzvah. The not-yet approach is equally applicable to those who have been observing Judaism for many years and to those who have just begun to incorporate Judaism, by stages, into their lives. It has inspired one rabbi to write:

> When someone who eats in a nonkosher restaurant orders beefsteaks instead of porkchops because he keeps kosher, I can no longer laugh at him. His choice was occasioned by a sort of low-level, yet very genuine, concern not to eat of impure beasts. . . . When he refuses butter on it and milk with his coffee because of "seethe not the kid in its mother's milk," I respect him further. And if he orders a scalebearing fish instead of meat, I see him struggling honestly to do God's will.[6]

All beginnings are difficult. Before I became observant, my parents sent me to an observant summer camp in northern Ontario. There for the first time I saw a community of observant

[6]Zalman Schachter, in *The Condition of Jewish Belief* (New York, 1969), p. 211.

Jewish young people, and learned the beauty of the Sabbath and the sanctity of the meal table. Upon returning home, I decided that I too would begin to observe the Sabbath and recite blessings before and after meals. But I worked piecemeal, and each week I added several new rituals to my mitzvah repertoire.

I recommend the same approach to those I teach and even to those who are in the process of converting to Judaism. For converts, feeling more Jewish each and every day is a continuous challenge. A Jewish identity is something that each of them has to build. As they continue to study and learn in a formal classroom setting, I recommend that they try to see each new day as an opportunity to do something Jewish.

A good beginning is simply to learn to use a Jewish calendar to measure time, noting the Jewish holidays and of course the time when the Sabbath begins each week. In addition, I recommend ongoing experimentation with Jewish ritual. Since Judaism is also a culture, visiting Jewish museums, reading Jewish literature, and seeing Jewish theater can further enhance one's knowledge of Jewish culture and increase one's feeling of Jewishness.

How Do I Become More Jewish?

Over the years, as a congregational rabbi, I have seen many people increase the level of their participation in Jewish tradition and culture. Following are some suggestions and guidelines which, in my experience, have often stimulated people to develop more dynamic Jewish lives. Remember, these are only guidelines for you to consider as a good beginning. And always keep in mind the not-yet approach.

The Sabbath and Other Jewish Holidays

Since Judaism is a family-centered, "hands-on" religion, it is never too late to begin to experience Jewish Sabbath and holiday celebrations, or even to initiate your own special traditions for the celebration of holidays. I began my home observance of Sabbath ritual when I decided that I would stay home and not use a car on Shabbat. You, too, may want to experiment on a given Sabbath by staying home and avoiding the use of car and television. At the least, this will enable you to rest and relax; and it will truly make the day different from all the other days of the week. Blessing food on the Sabbath and saying the blessing of washing the hands is another way to enhance home observance. Reading Jewish texts and allowing some time for study is also highly recommended.

Dietary Laws

The dietary laws have acquired a special significance because Jews in the past were prepared to keep them at the cost of their lives. In the time of the Maccabees, for example, the soldiers of Antiochus punished with death those who disobeyed the king's order to eat pork. As a result, over and above the natural abhorrence for the pig and the fact that the Torah forbids it, refraining from eating pork has become a powerful symbol of Jewish faithfulness even unto death. Since we must eat every day to survive, choosing what to eat and how to prepare it are an important part of our personal identity. For those who keep kosher, it teaches a measure of self-control and self-mastery.

Kashrut has proven the value of discipline, for by saying no to certain foods and by eating kosher foods, one develops the spiritual strength to resist other temptations. For those who respect life, there is the added benefit provided by the many controls that determine the humane slaughter of kosher animals. The reverence for live engendered by the dietary laws has contributed to the growth of a tradition that demands humane treatment of all living creatures.

Keeping kosher involves stages of observance. Do not consider yourself a hypocrite if you choose to observe only some aspects of the dietary laws. By observing these laws we rise in holiness and sanctify our lives. As with other aspects of Jewish observance, you are encouraged to advance along the ladder of holiness step by step. One level will likely lead to another, because in my experience observance leads to understanding and appreciation of the commandment. Your best bet is to consider all the possible choices, establish goals and priorities for yourself, and decide which options are feasible for you.

Prayer

Develop the habit of starting every day with prayer. The word for "prayer" in Hebrew, *tefillah,* literally means to judge or evaluate oneself. What better way to begin each morning than with a few minutes of self-appraisal and introspection. In addition, it is customary for a Jew to recite no less than one hundred blessings every day. Blessings help us to experience commonplace deeds as spiritual adventures. The most convenient place in which to find a listing of blessing possibilities is a prayerbook. Look for opportunities each day in which to say a blessing. (Several of my congregants carry blessing cards in their purses or wallets, and spend each day looking for opportunities to recite new ones.)

State of Israel

Israel is our second homeland. It is the birthplace of the Jewish people, where our spiritual, political, and religious identity was shaped. The Land of Israel has always been the focus of Jewish religious attention. The yearning to return to Jerusalem one day is a vibrant part of Jewish literature and prayer. "Next year in Jerusalem," recited at the end of our Passover seder and proclaimed at the end of Yom Kippur services, symbolizes the eternal longing of the Jewish people to visit Israel and its ancient capital, Jerusalem. (At the time of the writing of this volume, Jerusalem is celebrating its three-thousandth birthday!)

Some guidelines regarding Israel as part of your agenda include the following:

1.   Visit Israel whenever you can.
2.   Learn the issues in the Middle East conflict. Know the facts and read newspapers and magazines.
3.   Seek out political candidates who have shown a concern for the State of Israel.
4.   Give money. The United Jewish Appeal and State of Israel Bonds are two ways of supporting Israel. (There is always a need for volunteers to assist on Super Sunday, when money is raised by calling Jewish families throughout the United States on the telephone.)

Study

Because the Torah is considered to be the source of correct knowledge, studying it ranks as the highest commandment in Jewish law. The rabbis of the Talmud recognized study as one of the essential activities that ensured Jewish survival. When we study, we have the opportunity to appreciate our past, understand our present, and chart, to some extent, where we wish to go in the future. We can increase our Jewish vocabulary and skills, and better understand those which have always been part of our lives—thereby enhancing the meaning and power of rituals which often may have been done by rote. Study on a regular basis also gives us the opportunity to build strong foundations for the Jewish future.

Tzedakah and Deeds of Kindness

The Hebrew word *tzedakah*, inaccurately translated as "charity," really means "justice plus compassion." In Judaism, giving tzedakah is an act of justice. One who doesn't give it is acting unjustly. The highest degree of tzedakah, according to the philosopher Maimonides, is the person who strengthens the hand of a Jew reduced to poverty by giving him a gift or a loan, or entering into a partnership with him, or finding work for him, in order to strengthen his hand, so that he will have no need to beg from other people.

The term *gemilut hasadim*, "deeds of kindness," refers to a commandment that is performed with no expectation of reward. For instance, donating money to bury a poor person and giving money anonymously are examples of deeds of kindness in Judaism. Extending an interest-free loan is another example, or visiting the sick. Concerning deeds of kindness, the rabbis say that we will be rewarded by God in this world and rewarded a second time in the world-to-come (Talmud Shabbat 127a).

As teenagers, you will want to seek out opportunities to perform deeds of kindness. In most Jewish communities, there are helping organizations of various kinds that you are eligible to join. Here are some possibilities to investigate that could be in need of your help:

1. Jewish Family Service. Aids Jewish families with clothing, housing, and other kinds of monetary assistance.

2. Bikkur holim. Makes hospital visits.

3. Hevrah Kaddisha (Holy Burial Society). Assists in the preparation of the deceased for burial.

4. Free Loan Society. Usually part of the local Jewish Federation; provides interest-free loans to those in need.

5. Hakhnasat Orhim. Welcomes new families that have moved into the community, immigrant families, and so on. Arranges Passover seders for those in need of a place to go.

6. Social Action Committees. These groups, usually organized within a synagogue, work on various kinds of social action projects, e.g., providing food and clothing for local shelters, visitation to nursing homes and hospitals, helping to make minyanim, preparing food for bereaved families.

Being God's Partner

God-partnership is one of the great hidden themes of Jewish literature and Jewish life. The Book of Deuteronomy says, "Follow Adonai your God" (13:5) and "walk in all of God's ways" (11:22). These verses teach us that we should follow the attributes of God, which include being kind, merciful, forgiving, loving, speaking the truth, keeping our word and acting uprightly, and comforting those in need of comfort.

Hillel the Elder, who lived about two thousand years ago, is often quoted for his saying, "Never separate yourself from the community" (Pirke Avot 2:5). He is also noted for this saying: "If I am not for myself, who is for me? And if I am only for myself, what am I? And if not now, when?" (Pirke Avot 1:14). As Jews, we are always encouraged to involve ourselves with our people, to assist God, so to speak, in improving our communities and ultimately the world-at-large.

There is a Yiddish word which is untranslatable but describes the attributes of the kind of person that God had in mind when arranging for human creation. The word is *mensch*, and no doubt you have heard it before. To be a mensch is to be humble, reliable, honest, dependable, unselfish, kind, just, compassionate, and always sensitive to the feelings and needs of others. A mensch is a good person who always does things for the good beyond the letter of the law.

Make room for God in your life. Bring God in as your partner. God created us to be transformers and repairers, calling us to be a kingdom of priests. Like the priests of old, we too can light spiritual fires wherever we go. The Hassidim say that we human beings are God's language. May we, as God's language, continue to be God's partners in the unfolding process of creation. I wish you *hatzlahah rabbah*—much success in all you do in life!

Glossary

To be a knowledgeable Jew means to be familiar with certain key words, concepts, and values that have been part of Jewish life throughout the centuries. This glossary includes the terms that are presented in this book.

Bizui mitzvah: Religious commandment performed disrespectfully.

Bikkur Holim: Society organized to visit the sick.

Berit: Covenant.

Conservative Judaism: Branch of Judaism that maintains traditional view on law but holds that contemporary decisions should be fixed by rabbinic scholars and interpreted by local rabbis.

Chosen people: God's special selection of the Israelite people.

Derekh eretz: "The way of the land"; local custom, good behavior, courtesy, politeness, etiquette.

Ethics of the Fathers: Talmudic tractate containing pithy sayings and ethical teachings of rabbinic sages from third century B.C.E. to third century C.E.; also known as Pirke Avot.

Gemilut hasadim: Deeds of kindness.

Geneivat da'at: "Stealing a person's mind."

Hafetz Hayyim: Popular book on the sin of gossip; also, its author, Rabbi Israel Meir Hakohen Kagen.

Hakhnasat orhim: Welcoming the stranger, hospitality.

Halakhah: Jewish law.

Hevrah Kaddisha: Burial society.

Heschel, Abraham Joshua: Twentieth-century philosopher who attempted to illumine relationship between God and humankind.

Hiddur mitzvah: Beautification or adornment of religious commandment.

Hillel: Renowned sage of first century B.C.E.; sometimes called Hillel the Elder.

Hivvuv mitzvah: Performing religious commandment with love and affection.

Kavvanah: "Intention"; heartfelt direction in prayer.

Kiddushin: Jewish marriage.

Lashon hara: Evil speech, slander.

Lishmah: "For its own sake," as in study.

Maimonides: Medieval philosopher who formulated Thirteen Principles of Faith; also known as Rambam.

Mensch: A good person, one whose behavior reflects a high standard of values.

Midrash: Nonlegal sections of Talmud and rabbinic books containing biblical interpretations in the spirit of legend.

Mixed marriage: Marriage between Jew and non-Jew.

Mitzvah: Religious commandment or obligation.

Musar: Ethical guidance regarding proper conduct.

Nezikin: Fourth order of Talmud, dealing with money matters and damages decided by courts.

Orthodox Judaism: Branch of Judaism which acknowledges divine revelation of Torah and binding authority of Jewish law; also known as traditional Judaism.

Pirke Avot: *See* Ethics of the Fathers.

Reconstructionism: Branch of Judaism, founded by Mordecai Kaplan, which argues that Judaism is evolving civilization whose common denominator is continuous life of Jewish people.

Reform Judaism: The more liberal branch of Judaism; first modern movement to develop as a result of changes in Europe brought about by emancipation.

Revelation: Act of communication from God to humans; the content of such a communication.

Simhah shel mitzvah: Happiness deriving from performance of religious commandment.

Sinat hinnam: Gratuitous hatred (i.e., hatred for no clear reason).

Talmud: Rabbinic interpretation of Bible.

Tefillah: Prayer.

Tzedakah: Justice; righteous giving through charity.

UJA: United Jewish Appeal; organization that provides financial support for Jews in Israel and elsewhere.

Zerizut: Alertness in performing religious commandment.

Zohar: Book of Jewish mysticism.

For Further Reading

Dorff, Elliot N., *Mitzvah Means Commandment* (New York: United Synagogue Department of Youth, 1989)

Gold, Michael, *Does God Belong in the Bedroom?* (Philadelphia: Jewish Publication Society, 1992)

Isaacs, Ronald H., *Derech Eretz: The Path to an Ethical Life* (NewYork: United Synagogue of Conservative Judaism, Department of Youth Activities, 1995)

Olitzky, Kerry M. and Sabath, Rachel T., *Striving for Virtue: A Contemporary Guide to Jewish Ethical Behavior* (Hoboken, NJ: KTAV Publishing House, Inc. 1996)

Olitzky, Kerry M., Rosman, Steven M. and Kasakove, David P., eds. *When Your Jewish Child Asks Why* (Hoboken, NJ: KTAV Publishing House, Inc. 1993)

Salkin, Jeffrey, *Being God's Partner* (Vermont:Jewish Lights, 1994)

Summers, Barbara Fortgang, *Community and Responsibility in the Jewish Tradition* (New York: United Synagogue Department of Youth, 1978)

Wylen, Stephen M. *Gossip: The Power of the Word* (Hoboken, NJ: KTAV Publishing House, Inc. 1993)